D0594938

ROBERT N. ANTHONY
Harvard Business School

A REVIEW OF

Essentials of
Accounting

6TH EDITION

Prepared by
David L. Schwarzkopf
Bentley College

 Addison-Wesley Publishing Company

Reading, Massachusetts • Menlo Park, California • New York
Don Mills, Ontario • Wokingham, England • Amsterdam • Bonn • Sydney
Singapore • Tokyo • Madrid • San Juan • Milan • Paris

Publishing Partner: Michael Roche
Sponsoring Editor: Kate Morgan
Production Supervisor: Patricia A. Oduor
Composition: Jacqueline Davies
Text Design: Catherine L. Dorin
Cover Designer: Regina Hagen
Illustrators: ST Associates/George Nichols
Supevisor of Manufacturing: Hugh Crawford

The Coca-Cola® logo appearing on page 13 is a registered trademark of the Coca-Cola Company. Used with permission of the Coca-Cola Company.

The 7•UP® logo appearing on page 13 is a registered trademark of the Seven-Up Company. Used with permission of the Seven-Up Company.

Library of Congress Cataloging-in-Publication Data

Schwarzkopf, David L.
    A review of Essentials of accounting / prepared by David L
Schwarzkopf—6th ed.
        p. cm.
    Includes index.
    ISBN 0-201-44278-7 (pbk.)
    1. Accounting.   I. Anthony, Robert Newton, 1916–   Essentials
of accounting. 6th ed.   II. Title.
HF5635.A6879   1996 Suppl.
657—dc20   96-34146
                                           CIP

Copyright © 1997, 1993, 1988, 1985 by Addison-Wesley Publishing Company, Inc.

All rights reserved. No part of this publication may be reproduced, stored in a retrieval system, or transmitted, in any form or by any means, electronic, mechanical, photocopying, recording or otherwise, without the prior written permission of the publisher. Printed in the United States of America.

2 3 4 5 6 7 8 9 10 CRK 999897

Please Read This First

This book will help you teach yourself the essential ideas of accounting. You will learn what accounting information can—and cannot—tell you about an organization.

Accounting is the principal way of organizing and reporting financial information. Although there are differences in detail, the general structure and rules are similar in most countries and in most types of organizations.

Accounting has been called the language of business. Learning this language is complicated by the fact that many words used in accounting do not mean quite the same thing as they mean in everyday life. When using accounting words, it is important that you understand their accounting meaning.

As in any language, some accounting rules and terms have a single correct meaning, while others are like dialects in that their meaning varies with different users. You will learn to understand and allow for these differences.

How to Use This Book

This book is intended primarily for those who are studying, or who have completed, the programmed text *Essentials of Accounting* or its computer version, *Teach Yourself Essentials of Accounting*. It contains the complete text of every point made in that book.

You can use it either to review the meaning of an accounting term or to review an entire topic. Usually, the easiest way to review a term is to look it up in the Glossary. The Glossary gives a short explanation. If you want a longer explanation with examples, the Glossary will refer you to the proper page in the text.

If you want to review a whole topic, you can refer to the Table of Contents for the part and section in which the topic is discussed.

If you have been introduced to accounting by another book, you can review terms or topics in the same way. However, this book, as is the case with all accounting texts, is not by itself a satisfactory way of learning the subject. Students need the "hands on" experience that is provided by the programmed text or the computer.

Contents

Part 3
Balance Sheet Changes 21

Part 4
Accounting Records and Systems 35

Part 5
Revenues and Monetary Assets 47

Part 11
Analysis of Financial Statements 137

PART 1

Basic Concepts and the Balance Sheet

This part describes:
* The nature of the balance sheet.
* The accounting meaning of assets, liabilities, and equity.
* The first three of the nine concepts that govern all accounting:
  * The dual-aspect concept.
  * The money-measurement concept.
  * The entity concept.

Accounting is a language. The purpose of any language is to convey information. Accounting information is provided by reports called **financial statements**. This book will help you understand what the numbers in the financial statements mean and how they can be used. Exhibit 1.1 shows one of these financial statements; this report is called a **balance sheet**.

ELEMENTS OF THE BALANCE SHEET

A balance sheet gives financial information about an **entity**. The entity that Exhibit 1.1 refers to is Garsden Company. An entity is any organization for which financial statements are prepared. A business is an entity; a college, a government, a church, and a synagogue are also entities.

EXHIBIT 1.1

GARSDEN COMPANY

Balance Sheet
as of December 31, 1995
(000 omitted)

ASSETS		LIABILITIES AND EQUITY	
CURRENT ASSETS		**CURRENT LIABILITIES**	
Cash	$ 1,449	Accounts payable	$ 5,602
Marketable securities	246	Bank loan payable	1,000
Accounts receivable, net	9,944	Accrued liabilities	876
Inventories	10,623	Estimated tax liability	1,541
Prepaid expenses	389	Current portion of long-term debt	500
Total current assets	22,651	Total current liabilities	9,519
NONCURRENT ASSETS		**NONCURRENT LIABILITIES**	
Property, plant, equipment at cost	$26,946	Long-term debt, less current portion	2,000
Accumulated depreciation	−13,534	Deferred income taxes	824
Property, plant, equipment—net	13,412	Total liabilities	12,343
Investments	1,110		
Patents and trademarks	403		
Goodwill	663		
Total noncurrent assets	15,588		
		EQUITY	
		Common stock	1,000
		Additional paid-in capital	11,256
		Total paid-in capital	12,256
		Retained earnings	13,640
		Total equity	25,896
TOTAL ASSETS	$38,239	TOTAL LIABILITIES & EQUITY	$38,239

The balance sheet is a snapshot of the financial position of the entity as of one moment in time. The balance sheet for Garsden Company reports its financial position as of December 31, 1995. This date is the date to which the report applies and *not* the date on which it was prepared.

Thus, the heading tells three things:

1. The fact that the report is a balance sheet.
2. The name of the entity.
3. The date to which the report applies.

The Garsden Company balance sheet has two sides: the left, Assets, and the right, Liabilities and Equity. We will describe the meaning of each side.

ASSETS

An entity needs cash, equipment, and other resources in order to operate. These resources are its assets. **Assets** are valuable resources owned by the entity. The left side of the balance sheet shows the amounts of each of these assets as of a certain date. For example, the amount of Cash that Garsden Company owned on December 31, 1995, was $1,449,000.

Assets are resources **owned** by Garsden Company. Its employees, although usually its most valuable resource, are not assets in accounting, because the company does not own its employees.

LIABILITIES AND EQUITY

The right side of the balance sheet shows the sources that provided the entity's assets. As the heading indicates, there are two general types of sources, Liabilities and Equity.

Liabilities are obligations of the entity to outside parties who have furnished resources. These parties are generally called **creditors** because they have extended credit to the entity. As Exhibit 1.1 indicates, suppliers have extended credit in the amount of $5,602,000, as indicated by the item Accounts Payable.

Creditors have a **claim** against the assets in the amount shown as the liability. For example, a bank has loaned $1,000,000 to Garsden Company, and therefore has a claim of this amount, as indicated by the item Bank Loan Payable.

Because an entity will use its assets to pay its claims, those claims are against assets. They are claims against **all** the assets, not any particular asset.

The other source of funds that an entity uses to acquire its assets is called **Equity**. The name is Equity (singular) not Equities (plural), even though there are several sources of equity. There are two sources of equity funds: (1) the amount provided directly by equity investors, which is called **Paid-in Capital**; and (2) the amount retained from profits (or earnings)—that is, the amount of earnings that has not been paid to equity investors in the form of dividends—which is called **Retained Earnings**.

Creditors can sue the entity if the amounts due them are not paid. Equity investors have only a *residual claim*; that is, if the entity is dissolved, they get whatever is left after the liabilities have been paid, which may be nothing. Liabilities therefore are a stronger claim against the assets than equity.

We can describe the right-hand side of the balance sheet in two somewhat different ways: (1) as the amount of funds supplied by creditors and equity investors; and (2) as the claims of these parties against the assets. Both are correct.

DUAL-ASPECT CONCEPT

The assets that remain after the liabilities are taken into account will be claimed by the equity investors. If an entity has assets that total $10,000 and liabilities that total $4,000, its equity must be $6,000.

Because (1) any assets not claimed by creditors will be claimed by equity investors, and (2) the total amount of claims (liabilities + equity) cannot exceed what there is to be claimed, it follows that the total amount of assets will always be equal to the total amount of liabilities plus equity.

The fact that total assets must equal, or **balance**, total liabilities plus equity is why the statement is called a balance sheet. This equality tells nothing about the entity's financial condition; it always exists unless the accountant has made a mistake.

This fact leads to what is called the **dual-aspect concept**. The two aspects that this concept refers to are (1) assets and (2) liabilities plus equity, and the concept states that these two aspects are always equal. (This equality exists even if liabilities are greater than assets. For example, if assets in an unprofitable business were $100,000 and liabilities were $120,000, equity would be a *negative* amount of $20,000.)

The dual-aspect concept is the first of nine fundamental accounting concepts we shall describe in this book. The concept can be written as an equation:

$$\text{Assets} = \text{Liabilities} + \text{Equity}$$

This equation is fundamental. It governs all accounting. We can write a similar equation in a form that emphasizes the fact that equity is a residual interest:

$$\text{Assets} - \text{Liabilities} = \text{Equity}$$

For example, if the assets of Violet Company total $19,000 and its liabilities total $3,000, its equity must total $16,000.

The term "Net Assets" is sometimes used instead of "Equity." It refers to the fact that Equity is always the difference between Assets and Liabilities.

The amounts of an entity's assets and liabilities will change from day to day. Any balance sheet reports the amounts of Assets, Liabilities, and Equity at one point in time. The balance sheet therefore must be dated. From here on we shall use the term "19x1" to refer to the first year, "19x2" for the next year, and so on. Thus, a balance sheet as of December 31 of the first year is dated "as of December 31, 19x1." It refers to the close of business on that day.

Returning to Exhibit 1.1, if Garsden Company prepared a balance sheet as of the beginning of business the next day, January 1, 1996, it would be the same as the one in Exhibit 1.1, because nothing changes between the close of business on one day and the beginning of business on the next day.

MONEY-MEASUREMENT CONCEPT

If a fruit store owned $200 in cash, 100 dozen oranges, and 200 apples, you could not add up its total assets from this information, because you can't add apples and oranges. But if you knew that the 100 dozen oranges cost $5 a dozen and the 200 apples cost $0.40 each, you could then add these amounts to the $200 cash, and find the total assets to be $780 [= (100 * $5) + (200 * $0.40) + $200].

Thus, to be addable, amounts of different kinds of objects must be stated in similar units. The unit that appears in an accounting report is money, that is, dollars and cents. This is the **money-measurement concept**. By converting different facts to monetary amounts, we can deal with them arithmetically; that is, we can add one item to another, or we can subtract one item from another.

The money-measurement concept states that accounting reports only those facts that can be stated as monetary amounts. For example, the following facts could not be learned by reading a balance sheet of Able Company:

- The health of the company's president.
- Whether a strike is beginning at Able Company.
- How many automobiles Able Company owns. (The *number* of automobiles owned is not a monetary amount.)

Because accounting reports include only facts that can be stated in monetary amounts, accounting is necessarily an incomplete record of the status of a business and does not always give the most important facts about a business.

ENTITY CONCEPT

Accounts are kept for **entities**, rather than for the persons who own, operate, or otherwise are associated with those entities. For example, suppose Green Company is a business entity, and Sue Smith is its owner. Sue Smith withdraws $100 from the business. In preparing financial accounts for Green Company, we should record the effect of this withdrawal on the accounts of the entity.

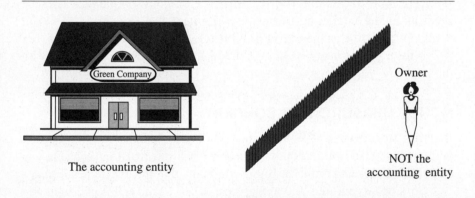

The accounting entity

Owner

NOT the accounting entity

If Sue Smith withdraws $100 from Green Company, of which she is the sole owner, Smith now has $100 more cash, but she has $100 less equity in Green Company. Smith is, therefore, no better or worse off than she was before. What about Green Company? It now has $100 less in assets. Thus, an event can affect the owner in one way and the entity in another way. Financial statements of Green Company report only the effect that events have on the entity. (Of course, Sue Smith can have her own personal financial statements.)

The fact that accounts are kept for entities as distinguished from the persons associated with those entities is called the **entity concept**.

Owners of some small retail stores (called "mom and pop" stores) may not identify the cost of merchandise they withdraw for personal use, personal telephone calls, and the like. If so, they do not apply the entity concept. Consequently, the financial statements of these stores are inaccurate.

A business may be organized under any one of several legal forms: a corporation, a partnership (two or more owners), or a proprietorship (a single owner). The entity concept applies regardless of the legal status. Municipalities, hospitals, religious organizations, colleges, and other nonbusiness organizations are also accounting entities. Although in this book we focus on businesses, the accounting for nonbusiness entities is similar.

KEY POINTS TO REMEMBER

- The assets of an entity are the things of value that it owns.

- The sources of funds used to acquire assets are (1) liabilities and (2) equity.

- Liabilities are sources from creditors.

- Equity consists of (1) funds obtained from equity investors, who are owners; and (2) retained earnings, which result from the entity's profitable operation.

- Creditors have a strong claim on the assets. They can sue if the amounts due them are not paid. Equity investors have only a residual claim.

- Total assets equal the total of liabilities plus equity. This is the dual-aspect concept.

- The amounts of assets, liabilities, and equity as of one point in time are reported on the entity's balance sheet.

- Accounting reports only those facts that can be stated in monetary amounts. This is the money-measurement concept.

- Business accounts are kept for entities, rather than for the persons who own, operate, or are otherwise associated with those entities. This is the entity concept.

PART 2

More About the Balance Sheet

This part describes:
* Two more of the nine basic accounting concepts:
  * The going-concern concept.
  * The cost concept.
* The meaning of the principal items reported on a balance sheet.

GOING-CONCERN CONCEPT

Every year some entities go bankrupt or cease to operate for other reasons. Most entities, however, keep on going from one year to the next. Accounting must assume either that (1) entities are about to cease operations, or (2) they are likely to keep on going. In general, the more realistic assumption is that an entity, or **concern**, normally will keep on **going** from one year to the next. This assumption is called the **going-concern concept**.

Specifically, the going-concern concept states that accounting assumes that an entity will continue to operate indefinitely unless there is evidence to the contrary. (If the entity is not a going concern, special accounting rules apply; they are not discussed in this introductory book.)

Because of the going-concern concept, accounting does not report what the assets could be sold for if the entity ceased to exist. On December 31, 19x1, the balance sheet of Hamel Company reported total assets of $500,000. If Hamel Company ceased to operate, we do not know what its assets could be sold for.

COST CONCEPT

When an entity buys an asset, it records the amount of the asset at its cost. Thus, if Mondale Company bought a plot of land for $10,000 in 19x1, it would report on its December 31, 19x1, balance sheet the item: Land, $ 10,000.

The amount for which an asset can be sold in the marketplace is called its **market value**. If you bought a pair of shoes a year ago for $75 and find that today you can sell them for $15, their cost was $75, and their market value is $15.

Some assets wear out. Inflation affects the value of some assets. For these and other reasons, the market value of assets changes as time goes on. Therefore, on December 31, 19x6, the market value of Mondale Company's land was probably different from $10,000. Accounting, however, does not attempt to trace changes in the market value of most assets. Thus, on its December 31, 19x6, balance sheet, Mondale Company would continue to report the land at its cost of $10,000.

The **cost concept** states that accounting focuses on the cost of assets, rather than on their market value. The cost concept is often called the "historical cost" concept, which emphasizes the fact that the numbers report what the entity *did* pay for the asset.

One reason why accounting is based on the cost concept is that it is difficult to estimate the market value of many assets. If you bought a pair of shoes for $75, the cost was clearly $75. However, if a few months later you asked two friends to tell you the market value of these used shoes, they probably would disagree as to the amount. Estimating the market value of each asset every time a balance sheet is prepared would be difficult. Furthermore, the estimates would be subjective, that is, affected by personal feelings rather than by objective facts.

A second reason for using the cost concept is that the entity will not sell many of its assets immediately. Instead, it will keep them to use in its operations. The entity therefore does not need to know their market value. This reason stems from the previous concept, the going-concern concept.

To summarize, the two reasons why accounting focuses on costs. rather than on market values, are that:

1. market values are difficult to estimate—they are subjective, whereas costs are objective; and

2. the going-concern concept makes it unnecessary to know the market value of many assets. The assets will be used in future operations rather than being sold immediately.

Examples. An entity bought land in 19x1 for $10,000. On December 31, 19x6, the entity received an offer of $20,000 for the land. This meant that the market value of the land was $20,000. However, this land would be reported on the balance sheet of December 31, 19x6, at its historical cost of $10,000.

A shoe store purchased shoes for $1,000. It expected to sell these shoes to customers for $1,500. Despite this, these shoes should be reported on the balance sheet at their cost of $1,000.

Accounting does not report what many of the individual assets are worth, that is, their market value. Accounting therefore does not report what the whole entity is worth. Those who criticize accounting for its failure to report an entity's "worth" do not appreciate that this task would be difficult, subjective, and unnecessary.

Some assets are recorded at what they are worth. If an entity has $1,000 cash, this asset is obviously worth $1,000. The market value of cash today is its monetary amount today. Cash is an example of a **monetary asset**. As we shall see in later parts, many monetary assets are measured at current monetary amounts, rather than at their cost.

BALANCE SHEET ITEMS

In the remainder of this part, we explain the meaning of some of the items on the balance sheet. Those not described here will be explained in later parts.

Refer back to Exhibit 1.1, which reports the amounts of assets, liabilities, and equity of Garsden Company as of December 31, 1995. The note "(000 omitted)" means that the numbers are reported in thousands of dollars. For example, the number reported for Cash, $1,449, means that the amount of cash was $1,449,000. This is common practice. It is done to make the numbers easier to read; users are not interested in the details of the last three digits.

Most items on a balance sheet are summaries of more detailed accounts. For example, the cash is probably located in a number of separate bank accounts, in cash registers, and in petty cash boxes. The total of all the cash is $1,449,000, rounded to the nearest thousand dollars.

ASSETS

In Part 1 we referred to assets as "things of value." Let's make this idea more specific. In order to count as an asset in accounting, an item must pass three tests.

The first requirement is that the item must be **controlled** by the entity. Usually this means that the entity must **own** the item. If Able Company rents a building owned by Baker Company, this building is not an asset of Able Company. The building is an asset of Baker Company. (Certain leased items, called capital leases, are assets. They are an exception to this rule. Capital assets are described in Part 8.)

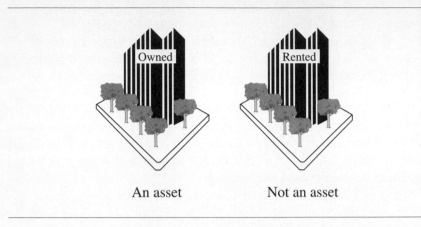

An asset   Not an asset

In accounting, the employees of an entity are *not* assets because the entity does not own them. However, if a baseball club owns a contract in which a player agrees to provide his services, the contract is an asset.

The second requirement is that the item must be **valuable** to the entity. Because of this requirement, the following items would not qualify as assets of a company that sells dresses even though they are owned:

*   Dresses that no one wants because they have gone out of style.

*   A cash register that doesn't work and can't be repaired.

The third requirement is that the item must have been acquired at a **measurable cost**. If Jones Company bought a trademark from another company for $1 million, this trademark would be an asset of Jones Company. By contrast, if Jones Company has built up an excellent reputation because of the consistently high quality of its products, this reputation would not count as an asset in accounting, even though it may be worth many millions of dollars.

> *Example.* "Coca-Cola" and "7•Up" are well known and valuable trademarks for soft drinks. The Coca-Cola Company developed the value of its trademark through its own efforts over many years. "Coca-Cola" is not an asset in accounting. Philip Morris, Inc., purchased the Seven-Up Company. Included in the purchase was an item called "Trademarks, patents, and goodwill," valued at $390 million. In accounting, "7•Up" is an asset of Philip Morris, Inc.

To summarize, for an item to be listed as an asset, it must meet three requirements:

1. It must be owned or controlled by the entity.
2. It must be valuable to the entity.
3. It must have been acquired at a measurable cost.

   Example. The following items of Homes Incorporated, a builder of houses, would not be among its assets:

   - Rented office space, said to be worth $200,000. (*not owned*)
   - Scrap lumber purchased for $2,000, but now worthless. (*not valuable*)
   - Its reputation for building fine houses, said to be worth $100,000. (*not acquired at a measurable cost*)

Assets and liabilities are each divided into two main categories, current and noncurrent. These are explained in the following sections.

Current Assets

Current assets are cash and assets that are expected to be converted into cash or used up in the near future, usually within one year. Groceries on the shelves of a grocery store are current assets. The store building is not a current asset. On the balance sheet, current assets are usually reported separately from other assets.

Cash is money on hand and money in bank accounts that can be withdrawn at any time.

Example. On January 8, Jones Company had $843 in its cash register and $12,012 in its checking account at the bank. Its cash was $12,855. On the evening of January 8, Jones Company deposited in its checking account $743 of the money in the cash register. After it had done this, its cash still totaled $12,855.

When an entity writes a check, the amount of its cash is not actually reduced until the check has been cashed. Nevertheless, the usual practice is to record a decrease in cash on the day the check is mailed.

Securities are stocks and bonds. They give valuable rights to the entity that owns them. The U.S. Treasury promises to pay stated amounts of money to entities that own Treasury bonds. Therefore, U.S. Treasury Bonds owned by Garsden Company are assets of Garsden Company.

Marketable securities are securities that are expected to be converted into cash within a year. An entity owns these securities so as to earn a return on funds that otherwise would be idle. Marketable securities are current assets.

Investments in safe, very short-term funds, such as money market funds, are often included in the cash item, rather than in marketable securities. The item is then called **cash and cash equivalents**.

An **account receivable** is an amount that is owed to the business, usually by one of its customers, as a result of the ordinary extension of credit. A customer's monthly bill from the electric company would be an account receivable of the electric company until the customer paid the bill. (The word "net" on the Accounts Receivable line means that the amount is less than the amount that customers actually owe. The reason for this is given in Part 5.)

If a customer signs a written **promissory note** agreeing to pay what is owed, the amount would be listed as a **note receivable**, rather than as an

---

CONSUMER NOTE

$ *400* XX   *July 1,*   19 *96*

FOR VALUE RECEIVED, ...*I, Fred Cochran,*.................................

promise to pay to.............*Ryan Lougee*...or order

the sum of.......*Four hundred* ———————————————..........Dollars

in......*one year*...from this date with interest to be paid ....*monthly*.............at the rate of......*12*....per centum per....*annum*....during said term, and for such further time as the said principal sum, or any part thereof shall remain unpaid.

Witness

Michael J. Vetere   *Fred Cochran*

FORM 306 REVISED 1959 HOBBS & WARREN, INC. PUBLISHERS, BOSTON   REVISED 1961 – CHAPTER 598

Secured by a Security Agreement (Chattel Mortgage) and a Financing Statement to be recorded in the Recording Office of the   or   County

☐ Secretary of State
☐ City or Town Clerk of
☐ Register of Deeds in the County of

---

account receivable. An example of a promissory note follows. Evidently, Garsden Company (Exhibit 1.1) did not have any notes receivable.

Inventories are goods being held for sale, as well as supplies, raw materials, and partially finished products that will be sold upon completion. For example, a truck owned by an automobile dealer for resale to its customers is inventory. A truck owned by an entity and used to transport its own goods is not inventory.

Prepaid expenses is the name for intangible assets that will be used up in the near future. (The reason for using the word "expense" will be explained in Part 6.)

A fire insurance policy that protects the entity against losses caused by fire damage is an asset, as is an entity's burglar alarm system, which also provides protection against loss.

Entities buy fire insurance protection ahead of the period that the insurance policy covers. When they buy the insurance policy, they have acquired an asset. Because the policy covers only a short period of time, the asset is a current asset. (Some insurance policies provide protection for more than one year; even so, they are often listed as current assets.)

An **intangible asset** is an asset that can't be touched. It has no physical substance. Insurance protection is an example of an intangible asset.

Noncurrent Assets

Assets that are expected to be useful for longer than one future year are called **noncurrent assets**.

Tangible assets are assets that can be touched; they have physical substance. Buildings, trucks, and machines are tangible assets. The usual name for tangible, noncurrent assets is **property, plant, and equipment**. Because they are noncurrent, we know that these assets are expected to be used in the entity for more than one year.

Exhibit 1.1 shows the cost of property, plant, and equipment to be $26,946,000. It also shows that a portion of the cost of this asset has been subtracted from the original cost because it has been "used up." This "used-up" portion is called Accumulated Depreciation and totals $13,534,000. After this amount is subtracted, the asset amount is shown as $13,412,000. This is the amount of cost that has not been used up. (In Part 8, we shall explain this amount further.)

The other noncurrent asset items are **intangible assets**; that is, they have no physical substance, except as pieces of paper. Rather than representing property, intangible assets represent property rights. The Investments item consists of securities, such as bonds. Evidently Garsden Company does not intend to turn these investments into cash within one year. If these securities were expected to be turned into cash within that period, they would be listed as a current asset, Marketable Securities.

Patents and trademarks are rights to use patents and rights belonging to valuable brand names or logos (such as "7•Up").

Goodwill, the final item on the asset side, has a special meaning in accounting. It arises when one company buys another company and pays more than the value of its identifiable net assets.

> *Example.* Grady Company bought Baker Company, paying $1,400,000 cash. Baker Company's identifiable assets were judged to be worth $1,500,000, and Grady became responsible for Baker's liabilities, which totaled $500,000. The following calculation shows the amount of goodwill:
>
> | | |
> |---|---:|
> | Baker's identifiable assets | $1,500,000 |
> | Less liabilities | −500.000 |
> | Net identifiable assets | 1,000,000 |
> | Grady paid Baker | 1,400,000 |
> | Therefore, goodwill was | $ 400,000 |

LIABILITIES

Current Liabilities

The right-hand side of the Garsden Company balance sheet lists the company's liabilities and equity, which can be regarded either as claims against the assets or as the sources from which the assets were acquired. The claims of creditors and other outside parties are called liabilities.

Consistent with the definition of current assets, current liabilities are claims that become due within a short time, usually within one year.

The first current liability listed in Exhibit 1.1 is **Accounts Payable**. These are the opposite of Accounts Receivable; that is, they are amounts that the company owes to its suppliers.

> *Example.* In December 19x1, Smith Company sold a personal computer to Brown Company for $3,000. Brown Company agreed to pay for it within 60 days. On their December 31, 19x1, balance sheets, Smith Company would report the $3,000 as Accounts Receivable and Brown Company would report the $3,000 as Accounts Payable.

The next item, **Bank Loan Payable**, corresponds to the asset Notes Receivable. It is reported separately from Accounts Payable because the debt is evidenced by a promissory note.

Amounts owed to employees and others for services they have provided but for which they have not been paid are listed as **Accrued Liabilities**. They will be described in Part 6.

Estimated Tax Liability is the amount owed to the government for taxes. It is shown separately from other liabilities, both because the amount is large and also because the exact amount owed may not be known as of the date of the balance sheet. It is a current liability because the amount is due within one year.

Two items of **Long-term Debt** are shown as liabilities. One, labelled "current portion," amounts to $500,000. The other, listed under noncurrent liabilities, amounts to $2,000,000. Evidently, the total amount of long-term debt is $2,500,000. The $500,000 is shown separately as a current liability because it is due within one year, that is, on or before December 31, 1996. The remaining $2,000,000 does not become due until after December 31, 1996.

Current Ratio

The current assets and current liabilities indicate the entity's ability to meet its current obligations. A measure of this ability is the **current ratio**, which is the ratio of current assets to current liabilities. For Garsden Company, the current ratio is:

$$\frac{\$22,651,000}{\$9,519,000} = 2.4 \text{ to } 1$$

If, in Garsden's industry, a current ratio of at least 2 to 1 is desirable, then Garsden Company passes this test.

Noncurrent Liabilities

As we have seen, Garsden Company has obtained funds by borrowing, and $2,000,000 of this debt is not due to be repaid until after December 31, 1996. This amount is therefore a **noncurrent liability**.

Suppose the $500,000 current portion was paid in 1996, and an additional $600,000 of debt became due in 1997. On the balance sheet as of December 31, 1996, the current portion of long-term debt would be reported as $600,000, and the noncurrent liability would be reduced to $1,400,000.

Although a single **liability** may have both a current portion and a noncurrent portion, a single **asset** is not always so divided. Prepaid Insurance of $2,000 covering protection for two future years is often reported as a current asset of $2,000.

The other noncurrent liability, Deferred Income Taxes, will be described in Part 8.

EQUITY

The equity section is often labelled "Shareholders' Equity" or "Owners' Equity." Equity consists of capital obtained from sources that are not liabilities. As Exhibit 1.1 indicates, there are two sources of equity capital: (1) $12,256,000, which is labelled "Total Paid-in Capital"; and (2) $13,640,000, which is labelled "Retained Earnings."

Paid-in Capital is the amount of capital supplied by equity investors. They own the entity. The details of how this item is reported depends on the type of organization. Garsden Company is a corporation, and its owners receive *shares* of common stock as evidence of their ownership. They are therefore called **shareholders** (or stockholders). Other forms of ownership will be described in Part 9.

The Paid-in Capital is reported as two separate amounts: $1,000,000, which is labelled "Common Stock," and $11,256,000, labelled "Additional Paid-in Capital." The reasons for this distinction are described in Part 9. The important number is the total amount paid in by the shareholders, which is $12,256,000.

Individual shareholders may sell their stock to someone else, but this has no effect on the balance sheet of the corporation. The market price of shares of General Motors Corporation stock changes practically every day, but the amount of Paid-in Capital reported on the General Motors balance sheet does not reflect these changes. This is consistent with the entity concept; transactions between individual shareholders do not affect the entity.

Retained Earnings. The other equity item, $13,640,000, shows the amount of equity that has been *earned* by the profitable operations of the company and that has been *retained* in the entity; hence the name, Retained Earnings.

Retained Earnings represents those amounts that have been retained in the entity after part of the company's earnings (i.e., profits) have been paid to shareholders in the form of dividends. In other words:

Retained Earnings = Earnings – Dividends

Retained Earnings are additions to equity that have accumulated since the entity began, not those of a single year. Therefore, unless Garsden Company has been in business only one year, the $13,640,000 shown as Retained Earnings as of December 31, 1995, reflects all previous years of operations.

The amount of Retained Earnings shows the amount of capital generated by operating activities and retained in the entity. It is *not* cash. Cash is an asset. On December 31, 1995, the amount of Cash was $1,449,000. The amount of Retained Earnings was $13,640,000.

KEY POINTS TO REMEMBER

- The going-concern concept: Accounting assumes that an entity will continue to operate indefinitely.

- The cost concept: Accounting focuses on the cost of assets, rather than on their market value.

- Assets are valuable items that are owned or controlled by the entity and that were acquired at a measurable cost. Goodwill is not an asset unless it was purchased.

- Current assets are cash and assets that are expected to be converted into cash or used up in the near future, usually within one year.

- Current liabilities are obligations due in the near future, usually within one year.

- The current ratio is the ratio of current assets to current liabilities.

- Marketable securities are current assets; investments are noncurrent assets.

- A single liability may have both a current portion and a noncurrent portion.

- Equity consists of paid-in capital (which in a corporation is represented by shares of stock) plus earnings retained since the entity began. It does not report the market value of the stock. Retained earnings is not cash; it is part of the owners' claim on the assets.

The following diagram summarizes how assets are reported. (It anticipates details described in later Parts.)

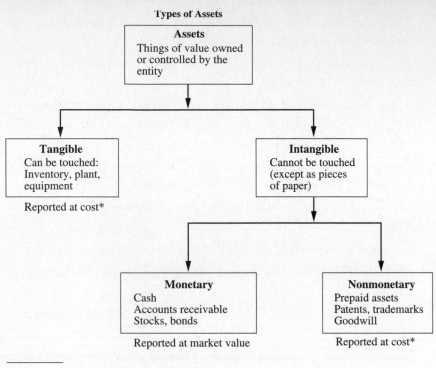

Types of Assets

Assets
Things of value owned
or controlled by the
entity

Tangible
Can be touched:
Inventory, plant,
equipment

Reported at cost*

Intangible
Cannot be touched
(except as pieces
of paper)

Monetary
Cash
Accounts receivable
Stocks, bonds

Reported at market value

Nonmonetary
Prepaid assets
Patents, trademarks
Goodwill

Reported at cost*

*Historical cost less depreciation or amortization

PART 3

Balance Sheet Changes

This part describes:

* How several types of transactions change the amounts reported on the balance sheet.
* The nature of income and the income statement.

ANALYSIS OF TRANSACTIONS

The amounts of assets, liabilities, and equity of an entity change from day to day, and the amounts shown on its balance sheet also change. Although a balance sheet must be prepared at the end of each year, it can be prepared more often. In this part, we will prepare a balance sheet at the end of each day. We will consider a business named Glendale Market, owned by a proprietor, John Smith.

Initial Paid-in Capital

On January 2, Smith started Glendale Market by opening a bank account in its name and depositing $10,000 of his money in it. Its balance sheet as of January 2 appeared as follows:

GLENDALE MARKET

Balance Sheet as of January 2

Assets		Liabilities and Equity	
Cash	$10,000	Paid-in Capital	$10,000
Total	$10,000	Total	$10,000

This balance sheet tells us how much cash Glendale Market had on January 2. The separation of Glendale Market from John Smith, the person, is an illustration of the entity concept.

An entity owned by one person, such as Glendale Market, is called a **proprietorship**. In some proprietorships, the equity item is labelled with the proprietor's name: "John Smith, Capital." This is simply a variation in terminology, not a difference in concepts.

To record the effect of this event on the financial condition of the entity, we made two changes in the balance sheet. After we made these changes, the balance sheet balanced. This is an illustration of the dual-aspect concept.

A total should always be given for each side of the balance sheet. Amounts on a balance sheet are generally listed with the most current items first.

Borrowing Money

When an entity borrows money, it may sign a written promise to repay. Such a written promise is termed a **note**. For example, if Business *A* borrows money from Business *B*, signing a note, Business *A* will record a note payable on its balance sheet and Business *B* will record a note receivable.

On January 3, Glendale Market borrowed $5,000 cash from a bank, giving a note therefor. Its balance sheet as of January 3 was as follows (items that were changed are shown in **boldface**):

GLENDALE MARKET

Balance Sheet as of January **3**

Assets		Liabilities and Equity	
Cash	**$15,000**	**Note payable**	**$ 5,000**
		Paid-in Capital	10,000
Total	**$15,000**	Total	**$15,000**

To record the effect of the event of January 3, two changes in the balance sheet (not counting the new totals and the new date) were necessary. The changes did not affect the equality that had existed between assets and liabilities + equity.

Purchase of Inventory for Cash

On January 4, Glendale Market purchased inventory costing $2,000, paying cash. Its balance sheet as of January 4 was as follows:

GLENDALE MARKET

Balance Sheet as of January **4**

Assets		Liabilities and Equity	
Cash	**$13,000**	Note payable	$ 5,000
Inventory	**2,000**	Paid-in capital	10,000
Total	$15,000	Total	$15,000

The event of January 4 required two changes on the balance sheet, even though only one side of the balance sheet was affected.

Each event that is recorded in the accounting records is called a **transaction**. Each transaction causes at least two changes on the balance sheet (not counting the changes in the totals and in the date), even when only one side of the balance sheet is affected. This is true of all transactions, and this is why accounting is called a **double-entry system**.

Earlier we described the fundamental accounting equation: Assets = Liabilities + Equity. If we were to record only *one* aspect of a transaction, this equation would not continue to describe an equality. The fundamental accounting equation was referred to in Part 1 as the dual-aspect concept.

Sale of Merchandise for Cash

When a business sells merchandise for $300 that had cost it $200, the profit of $100 represents an increase of $100 in equity. As we saw in Part 2, the Retained Earnings item is used to record changes in equity arising from the operation of the business.

On January 5, Glendale Market sold merchandise for $300, receiving cash. The merchandise had cost $200. Its balance sheet as of January 5 was as shown on page 24.

GLENDALE MARKET

Balance Sheet as of January 5

Assets		Liabilities and Equity	
Cash	**$13,300**	Note payable	$ 5,000
Inventory	**1,800**	Paid-in capital	10,000
		Retained earnings	**100**
Total	**$15,100**	Total	**$15,100**

We can analyze the individual parts of this transaction as follows: Glendale Market received cash of $300. Merchandise that had cost $200 was removed from its inventory. The transaction caused a net increase of $100 in the assets of Glendale Market from what they had been at the close of business on January 4. This increase was the result of selling the merchandise at a profit.

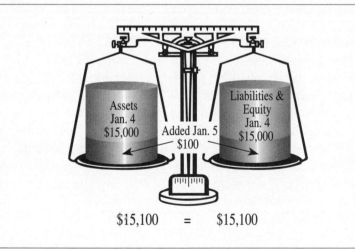

Purchase of Inventory on Credit

On January 6, Glendale Market purchased merchandise for $2,000 and added it to its inventory. It agreed to pay the vendor within 30 days. An obligation to pay a vendor is called an "Account Payable." Glendale Market's balance sheet as of January 6 was as follows:

GLENDALE MARKET

Balance Sheet as of January 6

Assets		Liabilities and Equity	
Cash	$13,300	**Accounts payable**	**$2,000**
Inventory	**3,800**	Note payable	5,000
		Paid-in capital	10,000
		Retained earnings	100
Total	$17,100	Total	$17,100

Cash Sale

On January 7, merchandise costing $500 was sold for $800, which was received in cash. The balance sheet as of January 7 was as follows:

GLENDALE MARKET

Balance Sheet as of January 7

Assets		Liabilities and Equity	
Cash	$14,100	Accounts payable	$ 2,000
Inventory	**3,300**	Note payable	5,000
		Paid-in capital	10,000
		Retained earnings	**400**
Total	$17,400	Total	$17,400

Credit Sale

On January 8, merchandise costing $600 was sold for $900. The customer agreed to pay $900 within 30 days. When customers buy on credit, the entity has an asset called "Accounts Receivable." The balance sheet as of January 8 was as shown on page 26.

GLENDALE MARKET

Balance Sheet as of January 8

Assets		Liabilities and Equity	
Cash	$14,100	Accounts payable......................	$ 2,000
Accounts receivable	**900**	Note payable	5,000
Inventory....................................	**2,700**	Paid-in capital	10,000
		Retained earnings	**700**
Total	$17,700	Total	$17,700

Purchase of Prepaid Insurance

On January 9, Glendale Market purchased a one-year insurance policy for $200, paying cash. Recall that the right to insurance protection is an asset. For this asset, we use the term "Prepaid Insurance." The balance sheet as of January 9 was as follows:

GLENDALE MARKET

Balance Sheet as of January 9

Assets		Liabilities and Equity	
Cash	**$13,900**	Accounts payable......................	$ 2,000
Accounts receivable..................	900	Note payable	5,000
Inventory....................................	2,700	Paid-in capital	10,000
Prepaid insurance	**200**	Retained earnings	700
Total	$17,700	Total	$17,700

Purchase of Land: Mortgage Payable

On January 10, Glendale Market purchased two lots of land of equal size for a total of $10,000. It thereby acquired an asset, Land. It paid $2,000 in cash and gave a ten-year mortgage for the balance of $8,000. Its balance sheet as of January 10 was as follows:

GLENDALE MARKET

Balance Sheet as of January 10

Assets		Liabilities and Equity	
Cash	**$11,900**	Accounts payable......................	$ 2,000
Accounts receivable..................	900	Note payable.............................	5,000
Inventory....................................	2,700	**Mortgage payable**	**8,000**
Prepaid insurance......................	200	Paid-in capital...........................	10,000
Land...	**10,000**	Retained earnings	700
Total	**$25,700**	Total	**$25,700**

Sale of Land

On January 11, Glendale Market sold one of the two lots of land for $5,000. The buyer paid $1,000 cash and assumed $4,000 of the mortgage; that is, Glendale Market was no longer responsible for this half of the mortgage payable. Its balance sheet as of January 11 was as follows:

GLENDALE MARKET

Balance Sheet as of January 11

Assets		Liabilities and Equity	
Cash	**$12,900**	Accounts payable......................	$ 2,000
Accounts receivable..................	900	Note payable.............................	5,000
Inventory....................................	2,700	Mortgage payable	**4,000**
Prepaid insurance......................	200	Paid-in capital...........................	10,000
Land..	**5,000**	Retained earnings	700
Total	**$21,700**	Total	**$21,700**

Valuation of Equity

On January 12, Smith received an offer of $15,000 for his equity in Glendale Market. Although his equity was then only $10,700 (Paid-in Capital of $10,000 plus Retained Earnings of $700), he rejected the offer. It was evident that the store had already acquired goodwill with a market value of $4,300.

This offer has no effect on the balance sheet. Goodwill is an asset only when it has been purchased. There was no transaction associated with this offer. Remember that the balance sheet does not show the market value of the entity.

Withdrawal by Owner

On January 13, Smith withdrew for his personal use $200 cash from the Glendale Market bank account and he also withdrew merchandise costing $400. Glendale Market's balance sheet as of January 13 was as follows:

GLENDALE MARKET

Balance Sheet as of January 13

Assets		Liabilities and Equity	
Cash	$12,700	Accounts payable	$ 2,000
Accounts receivable	900	Note payable	5,000
Inventory	2,300	Mortgage payable	4,000
Prepaid insurance	200	Paid-in capital	10,000
Land	5,000	Retained earnings	100
Total	$21,100	Total	$21,100

Market Value of Land

On January 14, Smith learned that the person who purchased the land on January 11 for $5,000 sold it for $8,000. The lot still owned by Glendale Market was identical in value with this other plot.

There is no effect on the balance sheet. Although the land still owned by Glendale Market may also have a market value of $8,000, accounting does not consider market values. There has been no **transaction** involving the Glendale Market land. That land continues to be reported at its cost of $5,000.

Repayment of Bank Loan

On January 15, Glendale Market paid off $2,000 of its bank loan, giving cash (disregard interest). Its balance sheet as of January 15 was as follows:

GLENDALE MARKET

Balance Sheet as of January 15

Assets		Liabilities and Equity	
Cash	$10,700	Accounts payable	$2,000
Accounts receivable	900	Note payable	3,000
Inventory	2,300	Mortgage payable	4,000
Prepaid insurance	200	Paid-in capital	10,000
Land	5,000	Retained earnings	100
Total	$19,100	Total	$19,100

Change to a Corporation

On January 16, Glendale Market was changed to a corporation. John Smith received 100 shares of common stock in exchange for his $10,100 equity in the business. He immediately sold 25 of these shares for $4,000 cash.

John Smith's sale of shares has no effect on Glendale Market's balance sheet. Although there is a transaction here, it is a transaction between John Smith and the person who bought his shares. Glendale Market was not involved. (The name of the entity may have been changed to, say, Glendale Market Corporation, but this does not affect the numbers on the balance sheet.)

Any conceivable transaction can be recorded in terms of its effect on the balance sheet, just as we have done in this section. Although we shall describe techniques, refinements, and shortcuts in later parts, none of them changes this basic fact.

EQUITY AND INCOME

Some of the transactions illustrated above affected equity; others did not. We shall now focus on the transactions that affected equity.

As explained in Part 1, an entity's equity increases for either of two reasons. One is the receipt of capital from owners. On January 2, Glendale Market received $10,000 from John Smith, its owner. This was recorded as an increase in Cash and an increase in the equity item Paid-in Capital.

The other source of an increase in equity is the profitable operation of the entity. Transactions that increase profit also increase the equity item Retained Earnings. In the following table, we show the dollar amount of the change in Retained Earnings, if any, that resulted from each transaction from January 3 through 8.

Date	Nature	Retained Earnings	
		Increased by	No effect
3	Borrowing		X
4	Purchase		X
5	Sale	$100	
6	Purchase		X
7	Sale	300	
8	Sale	300	
	Total	$700	

As can be seen from the table above, three of these transactions did not affect Retained Earnings: borrowing money and purchasing merchandise. The sale of that merchandise, however, did affect Retained Earnings.

The amount by which equity increased as a result of operations during a period of time is called the **income** of that period. We have just calculated that the total increase during the period January 2 through 8 was $700, so Glendale Market's income for that period was $700.

The amount of income and how it was earned is usually the most important information about a business entity. An accounting report called the **income statement** explains the income of a period. Note that the income statement is for a period of time, in contrast with the balance sheet, which is for a moment in time.

The $700 increase in Retained Earnings during the period is reported on the income statement. This statement explains *why* this increase occurred.

To understand how the income statement does this, let's look at the January 5 transaction for Glendale Market. On January 5, Glendale Market sold, for $300 cash, some merchandise that had cost $200. This caused equity (Retained Earnings) to increase by $100. This transaction consists of two separate events: (1) the sale, which, taken by itself, increased Retained Earnings by $300; and (2) the decrease in inventory, which, taken by itself, decreased Retained Earnings by $200.

Taken by itself, the increase in Retained Earnings resulting from operations is called a **revenue**. When Glendale Market sold merchandise for $300, the transaction resulted in $300 of revenue.

And, taken by itself, the associated decrease in Retained Earnings is called an **expense**. When Glendale Market transferred merchandise to the customer, the transaction reduced inventory and resulted in $200 of expense.

Thus, when Glendale Market sold merchandise for $300 that cost $200, the effect of the transaction on Retained Earnings could be separated into two parts: a revenue of $300 and an expense of $200.

In accounting, revenues and expenses are recorded separately. We can calculate the revenues and expenses for the period January 2 through 8 as:

Date	Revenues	Expenses
5	$300	$200
7	800	500
8	900	600
Total	$2,000	$1,300

We can now prepare an income statement. Its heading shows the name of the accounting entity, the title of the statement, and the period covered. The income statement reports revenues and expenses for the period and the difference between them, which is income:

GLENDALE MARKET

Income Statement
for the period January 2–8

Revenues............................	$2,000
Expenses...........................	1,300
Income	$ 700

As the name suggests, Retained Earnings refers to the amount of income that has been retained in the entity. On January 13, Smith withdrew $600 of assets for his personal use. This reduced Retained Earnings by $600. Retained Earnings therefore became $100, calculated as shown on page 32.

Retained Earnings, January 2	$	0
Income	+	700
Withdrawal	−	600
Retained Earnings, January 13	$	100

Assume that in the remainder of January Glendale Market had additional income of $800 and there were no additional withdrawals. Since Retained Earnings was $100 as of January 13, it would be $900 on January 31. Thus, the amount of Retained Earnings on a balance sheet is the total amount retained since the entity began operations.

The terms **profit**, **earnings**, and **income** all have the same meaning. They are the differences between the revenues of an accounting period and the expenses of that period. (Some people use the term **income** when they mean **revenue**; this can be confusing.)

In later parts, we shall describe various revenue and expense items, such as sales revenue, interest revenue, salary expense, and rent expense. These explain in more detail the reasons for the change in Retained Earnings during a period.

The two financial statements may be compared to two reports on a reservoir. One report may show how much water *flowed through* the reservoir during the period, and the other report may show how much water *was in* the reservoir as of the end of the period. Similarly, the income statement reports flows during a period of time, whereas the balance sheet reports status as of a point of time. Thus, the income statement may be called a flow report, and the balance sheet may be called a status report.

Note also that withdrawals by owners (which are called dividends in a corporation) are not expenses. They do not appear on the income statement and do not reduce income. They do reduce Retained Earnings.

Finally, if Smith sold his equity in Glendale Market on January 31, he probably would receive some amount other than the equity of $10,100. This is an illustration of the cost concept.

KEY POINTS TO REMEMBER

- Every accounting transaction affects at least two items and preserves the basic equation: Assets = Liabilities + Equity. Accounting is a double-entry system.

- Some events are not transactions; they do not affect the accounting amounts. Examples in this part were: a change in the value of land, "goodwill" that was not purchased, and changing the entity from a proprietorship to a corporation.

- Other events affect assets and/or liabilities but have no effect on equity. Examples in this part were: borrowing money, purchasing inventory, purchasing insurance protection, acquiring an asset, giving a mortgage, buying land, selling land at its cost, and repaying a bank loan.

- Still other events affect equity as well as assets and/or liabilities. Revenues are increases in equity resulting from operations during a period. Expenses are decreases. Their net effect is shown in the equity item called Retained Earnings. Equity also increases when owners pay in capital, and equity decreases when owners withdraw capital, but these transactions do not affect income.

- A sale has two aspects: a revenue aspect and an expense aspect. Revenue results when the sale is made, whether or not cash is received at that time. The related expense is the cost of the merchandise that was sold. The income of a period is the difference between the revenues and expenses of that period.

PART 4

Accounting Records and Systems

This part describes:

* The nature of the account and how entries are made to accounts.
* The meaning of debit and credit.
* Use of the ledger and the journal.
* The closing process.
* Items reported on the income statement.
* Accounting with the computer.

THE ACCOUNT

In Part 3 we recorded the effect of each transaction by changing the appropriate items on a balance sheet. Erasing the old amounts and writing in the new amounts would not be a practical method for handling the large number of transactions that occur in most entities. Instead of changing balance sheet amounts directly, in practice accountants use a device called an **account** to record each change. In its simplest form, an account looks like a large letter T, and it is therefore called a **T-account**.

The title of the account is written on top of the T. As a matter of accounting custom, the name of an account is treated as a proper noun; that is, the first letter is capitalized. This is how a T-account looks at the beginning of an accounting period.

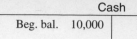

Cash		
Beg. bal. 10,000	

From this, we can tell the amount of cash at the beginning of the accounting period was $10,000. Note that although the amounts are in dollars, the dollar sign is not used.

Transactions that affect the Cash account during the accounting period can either **increase** cash or **decrease** cash. Thus, one side of the T-account is for increases and the other side is for decreases.

Increases in cash add to the beginning balance. Because the beginning balance is recorded on the left side of the T-account, increases in cash are recorded on the left side of the T-account. Decreases are recorded on the right side.

Example. The following changes in Cash are recorded in the T-account shown below:

   a. The entity received $300 cash from a customer.

   b. The entity borrowed $5,000 from a bank.

   c. The entity paid $2,000 cash to a supplier.

   d. The entity sold merchandise for $800 cash.

Cash			
Beg. bal.	10,000	2,000	(c)
(a)	300		
(b)	5,000		
(d)	800		

At the end of an accounting period, the increases are added to the beginning balance, and the total of the decreases is subtracted from it. The result is the **new balance**. The calculation of the new balance for the Cash account is shown below.

Cash			
Beg. bal.	10,000	2,000	(c)
(a)	300		
(b)	5,000		
(d)	800		
Total	16,100	2,000	Total
Balance	14,100		

The amount of the above Cash shown on the balance sheet at the end of the accounting period would be $14,100. The beginning balance of Cash in the next accounting period would also be $14,100.

RULES FOR INCREASES AND DECREASES

In the T-account for Cash, increases are recorded on the left side. This is the rule for all asset accounts; that is, increases in asset accounts are recorded on the left side.

Suppose Brown Company receives $300 cash from Ellen Jones to settle her account receivable. In the T-account below, the increase in Brown Company's cash that results is recorded on the left side as shown below.

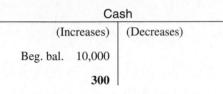

Ellen Jones, a customer of Brown Company, paid $300 cash to settle her account receivable. The Cash account increased by $300. Jones no longer owed $300, so the Accounts Receivable account decreased by $300. Accounts Receivable is an asset account. The dual-aspect concept requires that if the asset account, Cash, increases by $300, the change in the other asset account, Accounts Receivable, must be a decrease of $300.

The decrease in accounts receivable is recorded on the right side of the Accounts Receivable account. This balances the left-side amount for the increase in Cash:

```
                 Accounts Receivable
            (Increases) | (Decreases)
    Beg. bal.  2,000    | 300
```

Another customer of Brown Company settled an $800 account receivable by paying $600 cash and giving a note for $200. The effect on the accounts is as shown on page 38.

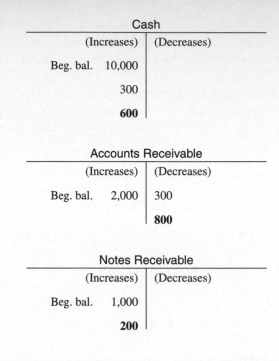

Cash

(Increases)	(Decreases)
Beg. bal. 10,000	
300	
600	

Accounts Receivable

(Increases)	(Decreases)
Beg. bal. 2,000	300
	800

Notes Receivable

(Increases)	(Decreases)
Beg. bal. 1,000	
200	

As you can see, accounting requires that each transaction give rise to equal totals of left-side and right-side amounts. This is consistent with the fundamental accounting equation: Assets = Liabilities + Equity.

An **increase** in any asset account is always recorded on the left side. Therefore, since the totals of left-side and right-side amounts must equal each other, a **decrease** in any asset must always be recorded on the right side.

> ***Example.*** Black Company borrowed $700 from Federal Bank, signing a note. Black Company's Cash account increased by $700, and its Notes Payable account, which is a liability account, increased by the same amount. The increase in Black Company's cash is recorded on the left side of its Cash account. In order to show equal totals of right-side and left-side amounts, the corresponding change in the Notes Payable account is recorded on the right side. These entries are as follows:

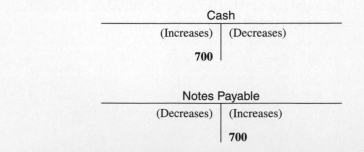

Cash

(Increases)	(Decreases)
700	

Notes Payable

(Decreases)	(Increases)
	700

Because left-side and right-side amounts must have equal totals, and because increases in assets are always recorded on the left side, increases in liability accounts, such as Notes Payable, are always recorded on the right side.

Similarly, because **decreases** in assets are always recorded on the *right* side, **decreases** in liabilities are always recorded on the *left* side.

As the equation Assets = Liabilities + Equity indicates, the rules for equity accounts are the same as those for liability accounts, that is:

- Equity accounts increase on the right side.

- Equity accounts decrease on the left side.

One way to remember the above rules is to visualize the two sides of the balance sheet:

Asset accounts are on the *left* side of the balance sheet, and they increase on the left side.

Liability and equity accounts are on the *right* side of the balance sheet, and they increase on the right side.

DEBIT AND CREDIT

In the language of accounting, the left side of an account is called the **debit** side, and the right side is called the **credit** side. Thus, instead of saying that increases in cash are recorded on the left side of the Cash account and decreases are recorded on the right side, accountants say that increases are recorded on the debit side and decreases are recorded on the credit side.

Debit and **credit** are also verbs. To record an increase in cash, you debit the Cash account. To record a decrease in cash, you credit the Cash account. Instead of saying, "Record an amount on the left side of the Cash account," the accountant simply says, "Debit Cash."

The rules we just developed in terms of "left side" and "right side" can now be stated in terms of debit and credit.

> **Increases in assets are** ....**debits.**
> **Decreases in assets are** ....**credits.**
> **Increases in liabilities are** ....**credits.**
> **Decreases in liabilities are** ....**debits.**
> **Increases in equity are** ....**credits.**
> **Decreases in equity are** ....**debits.**

In everyday language the word **credit** sometimes means "good" and **debit** sometimes means "bad." In the language of accounting, debit only means left, and credit only means right.

The word **debit** is abbreviated as "Dr." and the word **credit** is abbreviated as "Cr." In practice, these labels are not shown in the accounts, but we shall use them to help you fix them in your mind.

Because the total of the debit entries for any transaction should always equal the total of the credit entries, it is easy to check the accuracy with which bookkeeping is done. (We owe this ingenious arrangement to Venetian merchants, who invented it more than 500 years ago.)

INCOME STATEMENT ACCOUNTS

As we saw in Part 3, the income statement reports the revenues and the expenses of an accounting period and the difference between them, which is income. Revenues are increases in equity during a period, and expenses are decreases in equity.

For equity accounts, increases are recorded as credits. Because revenues are increases in equity, revenues are recorded as credits.

Similarly, decreases in equity are recorded as debits. Because expenses are decreases in equity, expenses are recorded as debits.

We can therefore complete the set of rules for making entries to accounts as follows:

- **Increases in revenues are credits.**

- **Increases in expenses are debits.**

THE LEDGER AND THE JOURNAL

A group of accounts is called a **ledger**. There is no standard form, so long as there is space to record the debits and credits to each account. Exhibit 4.1 is the ledger of Glendale Market, the same company we examined in Part 3.

EXHIBIT 4.1

GLENDALE MARKET LEDGER

Cash	
10,000	2,000
5,000	
300	
800	

Accounts Payable	
	2,000

Revenues	
2,000	300
	800
	900

Accounts Receivable	
900	

Notes Payable	
	5,000

Expenses	
200	**1,300**
500	
600	

Inventory	
2,000	200
2,000	500
	600

Paid-In Capital	
	10,000

Retained Earnings	
1,300	**2,000**

In practice, transactions are not recorded directly in the ledger. First, they are written in a record such as Exhibit 4.2, called a **journal**. The record made for each transaction is called a **journal entry**.

As Exhibit 4.2 shows, for each journal entry, the account to be debited is listed first, and the Dr. amount is entered in the first of the two money columns. The account to be credited is listed below, and is indented. The Cr. amount is entered in the second money column.

Journal entries are transferred to the ledger by the process called **posting**. The entries through January 8 have already been posted, as indicated by the check mark opposite each.

To summarize, any transaction requires at least two changes in the accounts. These changes are recorded first in the journal. They are then posted to the ledger.

THE CLOSING PROCESS

The Revenues account in Exhibit 4.1 shows increases in Retained Earnings during the period, and the Expenses account shows decreases in Retained Earnings. The difference between revenues and expenses is the net income of the period. The net income for the period is an increase in the equity account, Retained Earnings. Net income is added to this account by a series of journal entries called **closing entries**.

In order to do this, we first must find the balance in the account that is to be closed. The balance in the Revenues account in Exhibit 4.1 is $2,000 (=$300 + $800 + $900). An entry (shown here in boldface) is made that reduces the balance in the account to be closed to zero and records the same amount in the Retained Earnings account. Because the Revenues account has a Cr. balance, the entry that reduces revenues to zero must be on the other side; that is, it must be a Dr.

Therefore, the journal entry that closes the $2,000 balance in the Revenues account to Retained Earnings is:

```
Dr. Revenues.................     2,000
    Cr. Retained Earnings .....            2,000
```

Using similar reasoning, the journal entry that closes the $1,300 balance in the Expenses account to Retained Earnings is:

```
Dr. Retained Earnings........     1,300
    Cr. Expenses .............            1,300
```

These two entries are then posted to the ledger in Exhibit 4.1.

To get ready for preparing the financial statements, the balance in each asset, liability, and equity account is calculated. (Revenue and expense accounts have zero balances because of the closing process.)

EXHIBIT 4.2

JOURNAL

19x1		Accounts		Dr.	Cr.
Jan.	2	Cash	√	10,000	
		Paid-in Capital	√		10,000
	3	Cash	√	5,000	
		Notes Payable	√		5,000
	4	Inventory	√	2,000	
		Cash	√		2,000
	5	Cash	√	300	
		Revenues	√		300
		Expenses	√	200	
		Inventory	√		200
	6	Inventory	√	2,000	
		Accounts Payable	√		2,000
	7	Cash	√	800	
		Revenues	√		800
		Expenses	√	500	
		Inventory	√		500
	8	Accounts Receivable	√	900	
		Revenues	√		900
		Expenses	√	600	
		Inventory	√		600

Journal entries change the balance in the account. The *calculation* of the balance does not change the balance. Therefore the calculation of a balance does not require a journal entry.

The balance sheet is prepared from the balances in the asset, liability, and equity accounts. The balance sheet for Glendale Market as of January 8 follows.

GLENDALE MARKET

Balance Sheet as of January 8

Assets		Liabilities and Equity	
Cash..	$14,100	Accounts payable.......................	$ 2,000
Accounts receivable..................	900	Notes payable	5,000
Inventory....................................	2,700	Paid-in capital...........................	10,000
		Retained earnings	700
Total Assets	$17,700	Total Liabilities and Equity....	$17,700

The income statement is prepared from information in the Retained Earnings account, as follows:

GLENDALE MARKET

Income Statement
for the period January 2–8

Revenues............................	$2,000
Expenses	1,300
Net Income	$ 700

After the closing process, the revenues and expenses accounts have zero balances. These accounts are therefore **temporary accounts**. They are started over at the beginning of each period. The asset accounts have debit balances, and the liability and equity accounts have credit balances. These balances are carried forward to the next period. Balance sheet accounts are **permanent accounts**.

Most entities report individual items of revenues and expenses (such as salary expense, maintenance expense, insurance expense) on their income statement. In order to do this, they set up an account for each item. Thus, if the income statement reported 2 revenue items and 10 expense items, there would be at least 12 revenue and expense accounts. We shall describe these accounts in later Parts. The entries to them are made in exactly the same way as in the simple example given here.

Management needs more detailed information than is contained in the financial statements. For example, instead of one account, Accounts Receivable, it needs an account for each customer so that the amount owed by each customer is known. Therefore the ledger usually contains many more accounts than there are items on the financial statements.

Although you need to understand the bookkeeping process described in this part, you don't need to memorize the details. Our purpose is to show where the numbers in the financial statements come from. This helps you understand what the numbers mean.

A NOTE ON COMPUTERS

Most entities use a computer to do their accounting.The computer makes debit and credit entries according to exactly the same rules as those we have described. In this book, we necessarily show the journal entries manually because what goes on inside a computer is not visible. In a well-designed accounting system, the computer has the following advantages over the manual system we use in this book:

- The computer does not make copying errors. For example,when the computer writes a check, the amount of the check is always the amount credited to Cash and debited to some other account. The amounts reported on the financial statements are the same as the balances in the accounts.

- The computer assures that debit entries always equal credit entries. It will not accept an entry in which this equality does not exist.

- Once an amount has been recorded in the computer, it may be used for several purposes. For example, an entry to Accounts Receivable is used in calculating the total amount in the Accounts Receivable account, in the accounts of individual customers, and the amount reported on the balance sheet.

- The computer does not make arithmetic errors.

- The computer may require that certain rules be followed. For example, the credit entry for a check is always to the Cash account.

- The computer has built-in safeguards that help detect fraudulent or erroneous entries.

However, if the initial input to the computer is made by a person, an error made by that person may not be detected. For example, if a check is supposed to be for $962, and the bookkeeper keys in $926, the computer may not detect the error. (Some input errors can be avoided by the use of automatic input devices, such as scanners that read bar codes.)

Also, despite built-in safeguards, the computer cannot detect certain types of fraudulent entries. As examples of multimillion dollar errors reported in the press demonstrate, there is no guarantee that errors do not exist. Therefore, there must be an audit function to check on the possibility of fraud or error.

Although the computer may perform most bookkeeping functions, it cannot replace the accountant. The accountant specifies the rules to be followed in routine transactions, but, as we shall see, some transactions require judgment as to the accounts affected and the amount. The accountant must tell the computer how to make these entries. If the accountant makes an incorrect decision, the accounts will be incorrect.

KEY POINTS TO REMEMBER

- **Debit** refers to the left side of an account and **credit** to the right side.

- Increases in asset and expense accounts are debits. Increases in liability, equity, and revenue accounts are credits. Decreases are the opposite.

- For any transaction, debits must equal credits. For the whole set of accounts, debit balances must equal credit balances.

- Transactions are first recorded in a journal. Amounts are then posted to the accounts in a ledger.

- Revenue and expense accounts are temporary accounts. At the end of each accounting period, they are closed to Retained Earnings. Net income is the increase in Retained Earnings from operating performance during the period.

- The difference between the revenues of a period and the expenses of a period is the net income of the period. These revenues and expenses are reported on the income statement.

- Asset, liability, and equity accounts are permanent accounts. Their balances are carried forward to the next accounting period.

PART 5

Revenues and Monetary Assets

This part describes:
* The accounting period.
* What accrual accounting is.
* Three more of the nine basic accounting concepts:
  * Conservatism concept.
  * Materiality concept.
  * Realization concept.
* How revenue items are measured.
* How monetary assets are measured.
* The days' receivable ratio.

In Part 4 we introduced the idea of income. Income increases Retained Earnings. Retained Earnings is an item of equity on the balance sheet. Any increase in Retained Earnings is also an increase in equity. Net income results from the profitable operation of an entity. The amount of net income is one of the most important items of information that accounting reports. Net income is the difference between revenues and expenses. In this part we describe how the revenue portion of net income is measured.

ACCOUNTING PERIOD

An income statement reports the amount of net income over a period of time, which is called the **accounting period**.

For most entities, the official accounting period is one year. However, financial statements called **interim statements** usually are prepared for shorter periods. In Part 4 we prepared an income statement for Glendale Market for the period January 2 through January 8. This was an interim statement; the accounting period was one week. For most entities, the accounting period is the **calendar year**; that is, the year that ends on the last day of the calendar, which is December 31.

Some entities end their year when activities are at a relatively low level. For example, a school might end its year on June 30, when students have left for the summer. The accounting period for these entities is the natural business year. The period selected is called the **fiscal year**.

Entities don't fire their employees and cease operations at the end of an accounting period. They continue from one accounting period to the next. The fact that accounting divides the stream of events into accounting periods makes the problem of measuring the revenues and expenses for a single accounting period the most difficult problem in accounting.

ACCRUAL ACCOUNTING

On January 3, Glendale Market borrowed $5,000 from a bank. Its cash therefore increased and a liability also increased, but its revenues did not change. Revenues are increases in equity. The receipt of $5,000 cash from the bank on January 3 therefore did not change equity.

On January 4, Glendale Market purchased $2,000 of inventory, paying cash. This was an increase in one asset and a decrease in another asset. Since equity was unchanged, the payment of cash on January 4 was not associated with an expense.

On January 8, Glendale Market sold merchandise for $900, and the customer agreed to pay $900 within 30 days. This transaction resulted in no change in cash. Revenue was $900. This revenue was not associated with a change in cash on January 8.

The examples show that revenues and expenses are not necessarily accompanied, at the same time, by changes in cash. Moreover, changes in cash are not necessarily coupled with corresponding changes in revenues or expenses. Increases and decreases in cash are changes in an asset account. Revenues and expenses are changes in an equity account.

Many individuals and some small businesses keep track only of cash receipts and cash payments. This type of accounting is called **cash accounting**. If you keep a record of your bank deposits, the checks you write, and the balance in your bank account, you are doing cash accounting. Cash accounting does not measure changes in equity.

Most entities, however, account for revenues and expenses, as well as for cash receipts and cash payments. This type of accounting is called **accrual accounting**. Accrual accounting is more complicated than cash accounting, but accrual accounting does measure net income. Because net income, which is the change in equity, measures the entity's financial performance, accrual accounting provides more information than cash accounting.

In order to measure the income of a period, we must measure revenues and expenses of that period, and this requires the use of accrual accounting. In this Part, we describe the measurement of revenues. The measurement of expenses is described in later Parts. First, we introduce three more accounting concepts: conservatism, materiality, and realization.

CONSERVATISM CONCEPT

Suppose that in January, Lynn Jones agrees to buy an automobile from Ace Auto Company; the automobile is to be delivered to Jones in March. Because Ace Auto Company is in the business of selling automobiles, it would be happy that Jones has agreed to buy one. Although Jones is likely to take delivery in March, it is possible that she will change her mind. The sale of this automobile therefore is uncertain.

Because in January the sale of this automobile is uncertain, accounting does not recognize the revenue in January. If Jones does accept delivery in March, accounting recognizes revenue in March. This is a conservative way to account for the transaction.

Recognize revenue when delivered

Increases in equity are recognized only when they are *reasonably certain*. To be conservative, decreases in equity should be recognized as soon as they are likely to have occurred. Suppose an automobile was stolen from Ace Auto Company in January, and the company waits until March to decide that the automobile is gone for good. Conservatism requires that the decrease in equity be recognized when it is *reasonably possible*; that is, in January.

The **conservatism concept** therefore has two parts:

1. . Recognize **increases** in equity only when they are reasonably certain.

2. Recognize **decreases** in equity as soon as they are reasonably possible.

These are general ideas only. Specifics will be given in later Parts of this book.

MATERIALITY CONCEPT

A brand new pencil is an asset of the entity that owns it. Every time an employee writes with a pencil, part of the asset's value decreases, and the entity's equity also decreases.

It would be possible, theoretically, to find out each day the number of partly used pencils and to make a journal entry showing the amount of pencils that were used up and the corresponding "pencil expense" of that day. But it would be impractical to do this.

The accountant considers that the asset value of pencils was entirely used up at the time they were purchased or issued to the user. To do otherwise would be a waste of time. This solution is simple and practical, but less exact than the theoretically correct treatment.

The treatment of pencils is an example of the **materiality concept**. The materiality concept states that the accountant may disregard immaterial transactions. Material transactions are those that make a difference in understanding an entity's financial affairs. Deciding which transactions are material is a matter of judgment. There are no mechanical rules.

The other side of the coin is that the financial statements must disclose all material facts. For example, if a large fraction of a company's inventory is found to be worthless, the materiality concept requires that this fact be disclosed.

The materiality concept therefore has two parts:

- disregard trivial (i.e., unimportant) matters, and
- disclose all important matters.

REALIZATION CONCEPT

Consider an entity that manufactures goods and then sells them. In accounting, the revenue from these goods is recognized at the time they are delivered to the customer, *not* at the time they are manufactured.

Suppose that in 19x2 an entity delivers to a customer an item that it manufactured in 19x1. The revenue is recognized in 19x2.

19x1	19x2	19x3
Goods manufactured	Goods delivered	Cash received

Revenue
recognized

If a company sells services rather than goods, revenue is recognized at the time the services are delivered.

Goods (such as shoes) are *tangible* products. Services (such as repairing TV sets) are *intangible* products. Both goods and services are products. Thus, the general rule is that revenue from a product is recognized when the product is delivered.

At the time of delivery, revenue is said to be **realized**. The **realization concept** states that revenue is recognized (that is, recorded) in the period in which it is realized.

Examples. In January, Smith Company contracts to paint Herbert's house. The house is painted in February, and Herbert pays Smith Company in March. Smith Company should recognize revenue in February.

Gordon Company manufactures some imitation carrots in May. In June it receives an order from Peter Rabbit, Esq., for one carrot. Gordon Company delivers the carrot in July. Peter Rabbit pays the bill in August and eats the carrot in September. Gordon Company would recognize revenue in July, which is after the order was received and before the cash was received.

Revenue is realized when a *sale* is completed by the delivery of a product. Because of this, the word "sales" is often used along with revenue, as in the phrase "sales revenue."

A salesperson may say that he or she has "made a sale" when the order was written, even though the product is to be delivered at some future time. In accounting, writing a sales order is not a sale because the revenue has not yet been realized.

Revenue may be recognized (1) before, (2) during, or (3) after the period in which the cash from the sale is received. First, let's consider a case in which revenue is recognized in the same period as when the cash is received. For example, in January, Loren Company sold and delivered a motorcycle to Jerry Paynter, who paid $1,800 cash. In this example, revenue is recognized in the same month as the related cash receipt.

Next, consider this transaction: In January, Loren Company sold a motorcycle for $3,800 and delivered it to Jean Matthews. Matthews agreed to pay for the motorcycle in 30 days. In this case revenue is recognized in the month before the related cash receipt.

The revenue is accompanied by the right to collect the cash, which is an Account Receivable. Thus, the entry for the sale of the motorcycle on credit was:

```
Dr. Accounts Receivable......   3,800
    Cr. Sales Revenue ........          3,800
```

When the customer pays the entity for a credit purchase, the entity records an increase in Cash and a corresponding decrease in Accounts Receivable. Thus, when Loren Company receives a check for $3,800 from Matthews in February, Loren Company makes the following entry:

```
Dr. Cash....................   3,800
    Cr. Accounts Receivable ...         3,800
```

Revenue was not recognized in February.

Finally, consider the case in which revenue is recognized **after** the associated receipt of cash. In this case, the entity has an obligation to deliver the product. This obligation is a liability. It is listed on the right side of the balance sheet with the title **Advances from Customers**. (The terms "Deferred Revenue," "Precollected Revenue," and "Unearned Revenue" are sometimes used instead of "Advances from Customers.")

Example. In March, Maypo Company received $3,000 cash in advance from a firm to prepare an advertising brochure. Maypo Company would make the following entry in March to record this transaction.

```
Dr. Cash....................   3,000
    Cr. Advances from Customers        3,000
```

Maypo delivered the brochure in June. It therefore no longer had the liability, Advances from Customers. In June, it would record the entry:

```
Dr. Advances from Customers..   3,000
    Cr. Sales Revenue ........          3,000
```

The customer's advance may provide for revenue that will be earned over several future accounting periods.

Example. Suppose in 19x1 a publisher received $80 for a magazine subscription, with the magazines to be delivered in 19x2 and 19x3. The entry for 19x1 would be:

```
Dr. Cash.....................        80
   Cr. Advances from Customers              80
```

The amount of the liability at the end of 19x1 would be $80. The entry for 19x2 would be:

```
Dr. Advances from Customers..        40
   Cr. Sales Revenue.........              40
```

At the end of 19x2, $40 would be reported as a liability on the balance sheet.
The entry for 19x3 would be:

```
Dr. Advances from Customers..        40
   Cr. Sales Revenue.........              40
```

At the end of 19x3, $0 would be reported as a liability on the balance sheet.
Note that the effect of recording these transactions is to assign the total subscription of $80 to the years in which the magazine will be delivered—$40 to each year.

SERVICE REVENUE

Revenue is recognized in the period in which services are delivered. If a landlord receives cash from a tenant in January and in return permits the tenant to use an apartment in February, March, and April, the landlord recognizes revenue in February, March, and April. This type of revenue is called **rental revenue**.

Example. In January, a tenant paid the landlord $2,400 cash, covering rent for February, March, and April. The following table shows how much revenue the landlord would recognize each month and how much liability the landlord would report at the end of each month.

	Rental Revenue for the month	Liability at the end of month
January	$ 0	$2,400
February	800	1,600
March	800	800
April	800	0

When a bank lends money, it delivers a service; that is, the bank provides the borrower with the use of the money for a specified period of time. The bank earns revenue for the service it delivered during this period. This type of revenue is called **interest revenue**. In accordance with the realization concept, interest revenue is recognized in the period(s) in which the borrower has the use of the money. (The term "interest income" is sometimes used, but the amount actually is revenue, not income. Income is always a *difference* between revenue and expense.)

Interest revenue is similar to rental revenue. Banks deliver a service when they "rent" money; landlords deliver a service when they rent apartments. In both cases, revenue is realized in the period(s) in which the service is delivered.

To summarize, accountants recognize revenue *before* the related cash receipt by crediting Revenues and debiting an asset account entitled Accounts Receivable.

Accountants recognize revenue *after* the related cash receipt by debiting Cash and crediting a liability account when the cash is received. Revenue is recognized when the product is delivered in accordance with the realization concept.

There are exceptions to the principle that revenue is recognized when a product is delivered. They involve certain types of installment sales, certain long-term contracts, and a few other special situations. They are outside the scope of this introductory treatment.

AMOUNT OF REVENUE

The realization concept describes *when* revenue is recognized. The conservatism concept governs *how much* revenue is recognized.

Suppose Loren Company sold a motorcycle to James Austin for $3,000 on credit, but Austin never paid the $3,000. Loren Company's assets decreased by one motorcycle, but there was no actual increase in another asset. Therefore, Loren Company's equity actually decreased as a result of this transaction. Loren Company did not realize revenue from this transaction.

Obviously, if Loren Company knew in advance that Austin would not pay for the motorcycle, Loren would not have delivered it. Although Loren would not knowingly sell a motorcycle to someone who is not going to pay, experience indicates that some customers do not pay; in this case there is a **bad debt**. Loren must take this possibility into account in measuring its income. It does this by estimating the amount of revenue that it is *reasonably certain* to receive from all its sales during the accounting period. The conservatism concept requires that an entity recognize only the amount of revenue it is reasonably certain to receive.

Example. In 19x1 Loren Company sold $500,000 of motorcycles to customers, all on credit. It estimated that 2% of these credit sales would never be collected; that is, they would become bad debts. Its estimate of bad debts for 19x1 was $10,000 (.02 * $500,000), and its increase in equity in 19x1 was therefore only $490,000 ($500,000 – $10,000).

Loren Company recorded each sale as revenue at the time the motorcycles were delivered. In order to measure its increase in equity properly, it must decrease the total amount of the increase in equity by $10,000. Although this decrease in equity theoretically resulted from the overstatement of revenue, accountants record it in an account called **Bad Debt Expense**. The amount recorded as Bad Debt Expense would be **$10,000**. An increase in expense has the same effect on equity as a decrease in revenue.

After this decrease, the amount recognized as an increase in equity is $490,000. This is the amount that is reasonably certain to be realized. This is in accordance with the conservatism concept.

Since the Accounts Receivable account includes amounts from customers who probably will never pay their bills, it overstates the real asset value. Thus, if the Loren Company decreases its equity by $10,000, it must also decrease its Accounts Receivable account by $10,000. Otherwise, the equality Assets = Liabilities + Equity will not be maintained. However, accountants usually can't decrease the Accounts Receivable account directly because they don't know *which* customers will not pay their bills. Therefore, they set up a separate account, called **Allowance for Doubtful Accounts**. The estimated amount of bad debts is recorded as an increase in this account. Accounts Receivable, like all asset accounts, has a debit balance. Allowance for Doubtful Accounts, which is subtracted from Accounts Receivable, therefore must have the opposite balance, that is, a credit balance. The Allowance for Doubtful Accounts is called a **contra-asset** account, because it is subtracted from an asset account (Accounts Receivable).

The entry to record Loren Company's estimate that Bad Debt Expense should be increased by $10,000 and an Allowance for Doubtful Accounts of $10,000 should be established is:

```
Dr. Bad Debt Expense........    10,000
    Cr. Allowance for Doubtful Accounts  10,000
```

On December 31, 19x1, Loren Company had $125,000 of Accounts Receivable before subtracting the Allowance for Doubtful Accounts. Loren Company's December 31, 19x1, balance sheet would show:

Accounts Receivable, gross......................	$125,000
Less Allowance for doubtful accounts	–10,000
Accounts receivable, net..........................	$115,000

If sometime in 19x2, Loren Company decides it is never going to collect the $3,000 owed by Austin, it **writes off** the bad debt. It does this by decreasing Accounts Receivable and also decreasing Allowance for Doubtful Accounts:

```
Dr. Allowance for Doubtful Accounts 3,000
    Cr. Accounts Receivable ...                    3,000
```

Loren Company's equity in 19x1 was reduced by the estimated bad debts on sales made in 19x1, but its equity in 19x2 was not affected by this write-off of a bad debt. Since equity was decreased in 19x1, it should not be decreased again for the same motorcycle. The write-off had no effect on the "Accounts Receivable, Net" item on the balance sheet, because both gross Accounts Receivable and the Allowance for Doubtful Accounts are reduced by the same amount.

MONETARY ASSETS

Monetary assets are cash and promises by an outside party to pay the entity a specified amount of money. Examples are accounts receivable, notes receivable, and bonds owned by the entity.

Monetary assets are usually reported on the balance sheet at the amounts that are reasonably certain to be received. By contrast, nonmonetary assets, such as buildings and equipment, are reported at their cost.

DAYS' RECEIVABLES

Days' Receivables is the number of days of sales that are in Accounts Receivable at the end of the accounting period. Sales per day are total credit sales for the year divided by 365. The formula is:

$$\text{Days' Receivables} = \frac{\text{Accounts Receivable}}{\text{Credit Sales} \div 365}$$

Thus the Days' Receivables ratio, using the following data for Worley Company, would be:

Accounts receivable, December 31, 19x1 $ 50,000
Credit sales for the year 19x1 $365,000

$$\text{Days' Receivables} = \frac{\$50,000}{\$365,000 \div 365} = 50 \text{ days}$$

The Days' Receivable ratio indicates whether customers are paying their bills when they are due. If Worley Company expects customers to pay within 30 days from the date of the sale, the ratio of 50 days indicates that customers are not paying on time. (This is only a rough indication because it assumes sales are made evenly throughout the year, which is not the case with seasonal sales.)

KEY POINTS TO REMEMBER

- The official accounting period is one year, but financial statements can be prepared for shorter periods. These are called interim statements.

- Accrual accounting measures revenues and expenses during an accounting period and the difference between them, which is net income. Accrual accounting is more complicated, but more useful, than accounting only for cash receipts and cash payments.

- The conservatism concept: Recognize increases in equity only when they are reasonably certain; recognize decreases as soon as they are reasonably possible.

- The materiality concept: Disregard trivial matters, but disclose all important matters.

- The realization concept: Revenue is usually recognized when goods and services are delivered.

- If revenue is recognized before the cash receipt, an asset, Accounts Receivable, is debited (increased). If cash is received before revenue is recognized, a liability, Advances from Customers, is credited (increased). The liability is debited (decreased) in the period(s) in which revenue is recognized.

- The equity and accounts receivable balances in a period are reduced by estimated bad debt losses. A Bad Debt Expense account is used to record the decrease in equity. A contra-asset account, Allowances for Doubtful Accounts, is established on the balance sheet. When specific bad debts are later discovered, Accounts Receivable and the Allowance for Doubtful Accounts are reduced, but revenue is unaffected.

- Monetary assets are reported at the amounts reasonably certain to be realized, but nonmonetary assets are reported at cost.

- The days' receivables ratio is

$$\frac{\text{Accounts Receivable}}{\text{Credit Sales} \div 365}$$

It indicates whether customers are paying their bills on time.

PART 6

Expense Measurement: The Income Statement

This part describes:
* The difference between "expense" and "expenditure."
* How the expenses of a period are measured.
* The last of the nine basic accounting concepts:
  * The matching concept.
* The meaning of items reported on an income statement.
* Methods of analyzing an income statement.

In Part 5 we showed that the revenues recognized in an accounting period were not necessarily associated with the cash receipts in that period. If $1,000 of goods were delivered to a customer in August, and the customer paid cash for these goods in September, revenue would be recognized in August.

Revenues are increases in equity during an accounting period. Expenses are decreases in equity during an accounting period. Just as revenues in a period are not necessarily the same as cash receipts in that period, the expenses of a period are not necessarily the same as the cash payments in that period.

EXPENSE AND EXPENDITURE

When an entity acquires goods or services, it makes an **expenditure**. If in August Mogul Shop purchased goods for its inventory at a cost of $1,000, paying cash, it had an expenditure of $1,000 in August. It would record this transaction with the following journal entry:

```
Dr. Inventory...............    1,000
    Cr. Cash ................              1,000
```

If in August Mogul Shop purchased $2,000 of goods for inventory, agreeing to pay in 30 days, it had an expenditure of $2,000 in August. Accounts Payable, which is a liability account, increased. Mogul would record this transaction with the following journal entry:

```
Dr. Inventory...............    2,000
    Cr. Accounts Payable ......            2,000
```

Thus, an expenditure results either in a decrease in the asset Cash or an increase in a liability, such as Accounts Payable. (Occasionally an expenditure results in a decrease in an asset other than Cash. For example, when an old automobile is traded in for a new automobile, part of the expenditure is the decrease in the asset, Automobiles.)

Mogul Shop had expenditures of $3,000 in August for the purchase of goods for inventory (= $1,000 + $2,000). If $500 of these goods were sold in August, there was an **expense** in August of $500. The remaining $2,500 of goods are still in inventory at the end of August; they therefore are an **asset**. Thus, the expenditures of a period are either expenses of the period or assets at the end of the period.

Examples. If Mogul Shop sold the remaining $2,500 of goods in September, it had an expense of $2,500 in September, but it did not have any expenditure for these goods in September.

If in August Mogul Shop paid an employee $2,000 cash for services rendered in August, then it had both an expense and an expenditure of $2,000 for labor services in August.

When an asset is used up or consumed in the operations of the business, an expense is incurred. Thus, an asset gives rise to an expenditure when it is acquired, and to an expense when it is consumed.

Example. Irwin Company purchased a supply of fuel oil in 19x1, paying $10,000 cash. No fuel oil was consumed in 19x1. In 19x2, $8,000 of fuel oil was consumed, and in 19x3, $2,000 was consumed. There was an expenditure in 19x1, and there were expenses in 19x2 and 19x3.

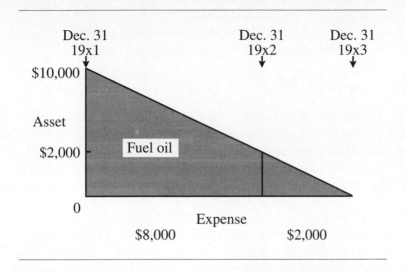

Between the time of their purchase and the time of their consumption, the resources of a business are assets. Thus, when fuel oil is purchased, there is an expenditure. The fuel oil is an asset until consumed. When consumed, it becomes an expense.

Example. Assume Irwin Company purchased a two-year supply of fuel oil in 19x1 paying $10,000. None of it was consumed in 19x1, $8,000 was consumed during 19x2, and $2,000 in 19x3. The balance sheet item for the asset Fuel Oil Inventory will show the following amounts:

As of December 31, 19x1	$10,000
As of December 31, 19x2	$ 2,000
As of December 31, 19x3	$ 0

The item Fuel Oil Expense on the income statements will be as follows:

For the year 19x1	$ 0
For the year 19x2	$8,000
For the year 19x3	$2,000

Over the life of a business, most expenditures will become expenses, but in a single accounting period, expenses are not necessarily the same as expenditures.

UNEXPIRED AND EXPIRED COSTS

Expenditures result in costs. When inventory or other assets are acquired, they are recorded at their acquisition cost. Expenses are the cost of the resources used up in an accounting period. Costs that are represented by resources on hand at the end of the period are assets.

Costs that have been consumed are gone; they have **expired**. Costs of resources still on hand are **unexpired**. You will find it useful to think of expenses as expired costs and assets as unexpired costs.

MATCHING CONCEPT

As we learned in Part 5, the concept governing the recognition of revenues of a period is the realization concept, which states that revenue is recognized in the period in which goods or services are delivered.

The concept governing the recognition of expenses of a period is the **matching concept**. It states that *costs associated with the revenues of a period are expenses of that period.*

> **Example.** Consider an automobile that Bryan Company, an automobile dealer, purchased for $15,000 in March and sold (i.e., delivered) for $18,000 in May. At the end of March, the automobile was in the Bryan Company inventory, so its cost was unexpired. At the end of April, its cost was still unexpired. In May, Bryan Company recognizes $18,000 of revenue from the sale of this automobile. It must match the $15,000 of cost with this revenue. Thus, its expense in May is $15,000. The $18,000 of revenue and the $15,000 of expense relate to the same automobile. The expense **matches** the revenue.

OTHER ASSETS THAT WILL BECOME EXPENSES

When products are delivered, their costs are matched with revenues in the period in which the sale takes place. These costs become expenses of that period. This is one application of the matching concept. Other costs associated with activities of the current period are also expenses, even though they are not directly related to the products delivered in the period.

If expenditures were made in an earlier period, the unexpired costs are assets until the period in which the expense is recognized. We shall consider several examples. The first is an intangible asset.

The general name for intangible assets that will become expenses in a future period is **prepaid expenses**. The asset account may identify the particular type of prepaid expense. Thus, the name of the asset account that shows the cost incurred for insurance protection in future periods is Prepaid Insurance.

Example. Bryan Company purchased a two-year insurance policy on December 31, 19x1, for $2,000. The effect of this expenditure is a decrease in Cash and an increase in the asset, Prepaid Insurance.

```
Dr. Prepaid Insurance........   2,000
    Cr. Cash................            2,000
```

During 19x2 Bryan Company used up half of this insurance protection, thereby incurring $1,000 of insurance expense. The effect on the accounts in 19x2 is a decrease in the asset, Prepaid Insurance, and an increase in Insurance Expense.

```
Dr. Insurance Expense........   1,000
    Cr. Prepaid Insurance.....          1,000
```

On December 31, 19x2, the balance in the asset account, Prepaid Insurance, was $1,000.

During 19x3 Bryan Company received the remaining $1,000 of insurance protection.

```
Dr. Insurance Expense........   1,000
    Cr. Prepaid Insurance.....          1,000
```

On December 31, 19x3, the amount of insurance protection has completely expired. The balance in the Prepaid Insurance account on that date therefore was zero.

Buildings and equipment also benefit future periods. They are assets like Prepaid Insurance and Prepaid Rent, except that they have a longer life and therefore benefit more future periods. The amount reported as an asset on the balance sheet is the unexpired cost as of the balance sheet date. Also, as with insurance and rent, the amount of building and equipment cost that is reported as an expense in each period is the amount of expired cost in that period.

The expired cost for buildings and equipment is called **Depreciation Expense**. If Bryan Company bought a machine for $5,000 and expected it to provide service for five years, the amount of expired cost in each year would be 1/5 of $5,000. In each of the five years Depreciation Expense would be reported as $1,000. Accounting for depreciation is discussed further in Part 8.

EXPENSES THAT CREATE LIABILITIES

We have described expenditures that first were assets and then became expenses as the costs expired. We now describe expenses for which the related expenditures are liabilities.

Amounts earned by the employees of Eastman Company for services performed in 19x1 are expenses of 19x1. If Eastman paid its employees one week after the week they worked, the amounts earned in the last week of 19x1 would be a cash disbursement in 19x2.

Assume that employees of Eastman Company earned $10,000 in the last week of 19x1, for which they were paid in 19x2. The $10,000 was both an expense and expenditure in 19x1. Eastman Company would report a liability of $10,000 on its December 31, 19x1, balance sheet.

Liabilities for expenses incurred but not yet paid for are called **accrued liabilities**. Account titles may describe the nature of the liability, in this case Accrued Salaries.

```
Dr. Salary Expense...........  10,000
     Cr. Accrued Salaries......          10,000
```

Employees are not paid the total amount that they earn. Part of their salary is withheld by the employer, who pays it to the federal government for income taxes. Amounts are also deducted for social security taxes and for other reasons. We shall disregard these complications and assume that total earnings are paid in cash to the employees.

Assume that in January 19x2, Eastman Company employees were paid the $10,000 owed them for work done in 19x1. This payment decreases the liability Accrued Salaries. The journal entry for this transaction is:

```
Dr. Accrued Salaries.........  10,000
     Cr. Cash.................          10,000
```

Fringe Benefits

Many companies agree to pay employees a pension when they retire. Employees earn the right to their pension benefits when they work. Therefore, if an employee earns a $2,000 pension benefit in 19x1 because he or she worked in 19x1, the $2,000 is an expense in 19x1. It is also a liability in 19x1. The liability is called Accrued Pensions.

Example. Joan Eaton earned a pension benefit of $2,000 in 19x1. The journal entry for this transaction is:

```
Dr. Pension Expense..........   2,000
     Cr. Accrued Pensions......           2,000
```

Joan Eaton retired in 19x7. She was paid a pension of $6,000 in 19x8. The journal entry for the 19x8 payment is:

```
Dr. Accrued Pensions........    6,000
    Cr. Cash.................            6,000
```

Most companies transfer amounts earned for pensions to an insurance company or bank, which makes the actual payments. The effect on the company's financial position is nevertheless the same as that illustrated in the above journal entries.

Many companies agree to pay for health care or other benefits to retired employees. These fringe benefits are called **Other Post-Employment Benefits**, which is often abbreviated to the initials OPEB. OPEB are accounted for in the same way as pensions; that is, the expense is incurred in the years in which the employee earns the right to them. The liability is also incurred in the years in which the employee earns the right to the benefits. When the benefits are paid, there is no expense.

Rent Expense

Eastman Company will pay its December rent of $5,000 in January. In December 19x1, it records the Rent Expense of December and the related liability, Accrued Rent, by the following journal entry:

```
Dr. Rent Expense............    5,000
    Cr. Accrued Rent.........            5,000
```

If in January 19x2, Eastman Company paid $5,000 to its landlord for the December 19x1 rent, the journal entry in January is:

```
Dr. Accrued Rent............    5,000
    Cr. Cash.................            5,000
```

Earlier we saw that if rent is paid *prior to* the period in which the expense was incurred, the amount is first debited to Prepaid Rent, which is an asset account. As the above indicates, if rent is paid *after* the period in which the expense was incurred, the entry is made to Accrued Rent, which is a liability account.

Prepaid expenses are turned into expenses by a debit to the expense account and a credit to the asset account. Accrued Liabilities are discharged by a debit to Accrued Liabilities and a credit to Cash.

Of course, many items of expense are paid for in cash during the accounting period. Salaries of $90,000 earned in 19x1 and paid in cash in 19x1 are recorded in the following entry.

```
Dr. Salaries Expense........    90,000
    Cr. Cash.................            90,000
```

LOSSES

Assets provide benefits to future periods. Suppose Bryan Company owned an uninsured machine that was destroyed by fire in 19x1. The machine will not benefit future periods. The asset amount carried for the machine therefore expired in 19x1, and this amount is recorded as an expense in 19x1. Thus, even though an asset does not provide benefits during a period, it is an expense of that period if its cost has expired for any reason. Such expenses are called **losses**. A loss is recorded as an expense in the period in which the loss occurs.

A loss is recorded as an expense if it is **reasonably possible** that the loss occurred, even though it is not certain. Thus, if a customer sues Bryan Company in 19x1, and if it seems reasonably possible that Bryan Company will lose the law suit, the estimated loss is recorded as an expense in 19x1. This is in accordance with the conservatism concept, which requires expenses to be recognized when they are reasonably possible.

SUMMARY OF MATCHING CONCEPT

Three types of costs are expenses of the current period. The period in which revenues are recognized is determined first, according to the principles described in Part 5. Then the associated costs are matched with those revenues. Costs are matched against revenues, not vice versa.

First, there are the costs of the goods and services that are *delivered* in the current period and whose revenues are recognized in that period.

Second, there are costs that are *associated with activities of the period*. The expenditures for these costs were made either in the current period or in an earlier period. If made in an earlier period, these amounts are assets on the balance sheet as of the beginning of the current period.

Third, there are *losses* that are recognized in the current period. These may recognize a reasonably possible decrease in an asset because of fire, theft, or other reasons. Or, they may recognize a reasonably possible increase in a liability arising from events occurring in the period, such as a law suit.

The cash payments associated with any of these expenses may have been made in a prior period, or in the current period, or they may be made in a future period, when the liabilities are paid.

The balance sheet at the beginning of a period reports assets obtained as a result of expenditures made in earlier periods. Part of these assets will expire and therefore are expenses of the current period. The remainder will be carried forward to future periods and will be reported as assets on the balance sheet at the end of the current period.

AN EXAMPLE OF MATCHING

Homes, Inc., is a company that buys and sells houses. Exhibit 6.1 describes some of its transactions during May, June, and July. These events relate to the sale of two houses, House *A* and House *B*. We will measure the income for Homes, Inc., for the month of June.

Delivery of the deed to a house is delivery of the ownership of the house. Exhibit 6.1 states that for House *A* this happened in June; therefore, revenue from the sale of House *A* is recognized in June.

The amount of revenue for House *A* is measured by two transactions:

Date	Transaction	Amount
May 2	Down payment	$ 16,000
June 5	Final payment	144,000
	Revenue from House *A*	$160,000

Certain costs are associated with the total revenue from the sale of House *A* of $160,000 in June. One of these costs was the cost of House *A*, which was $140,000.

Two of the cash payments related specifically to the sale of House *A*:

Date	Transaction	Amount
May 15	Commission	$ 800
July 2	Commission	7,200
	Total	$8,000

The **matching** concept requires that the costs associated with the revenues of a period be recognized as expenses of that period. Therefore, the two commissions associated with House *A*, totaling $8,000, should be recognized as expenses in June, even though they were not paid in that month.

In accordance with the realization concept, the $24,000 down payment received on House *B* in June was not revenue in June. It will be revenue in July. Because Homes, Inc., has an obligation to deliver the house, the $24,000 is a liability on the balance sheet at the end of June.

The matching concept says that general costs of operations during any period are expenses of that period. Thus the $4,000 general costs of operations in June are expenses in June.

EXHIBIT 6.1

TRANSACTIONS OF HOMES, INC.

Date	Event	Effects on Cash
May 2	Able agrees to buy House A from Homes, Inc., and makes a $16,000 down payment.	increase $16,000
May 15	Homes, Inc., pays $800 commission to the salesperson who sold House A (5% of cash received).	decrease $800
May	Homes, Inc., general expenses for May were $4,400 (assume for simplicity these were paid in cash in May).	decrease $4,400
June 2	Baker agrees to buy House B, and makes a $24,000 down payment.	increase $24,000
June 5	Able completes the purchase of House A, paying $144,000 cash. Homes, Inc., delivers the deed to Able thereby delivering ownership of the house. (House A cost Homes, Inc., $140,000.)	increase $144,000
June 30	Homes, Inc., pays $1,200 commission to the salesperson who sold House B.	decrease $1,200
June	Homes, Inc., general expenses for June were $4,000.	decrease $4,000
July 2	Homes, Inc., pays $7,200 additional commission to the salesperson who sold House A.	decrease $7,200
July 3	Baker completes the purchase of House B, paying $216,000 cash. Homes, Inc., delivers the deed to Baker, thereby delivering ownership of the house. (House B costs Homes, Inc., $200,000.)	increase $216,000
July 30	Homes, Inc., pays $10,800 commission to the salesperson who sold House B.	decrease $10,800
July	Homes, Inc., general expenses for July were $4,800.	decrease $4,800

The income statement for Homes, Inc., for the month of June, applying the realization concept and the matching concept, follows.

HOMES, INC.

Income Statement for June

Sales revenue .... $160,000 (= $16,000 + $144,000)

Expenses:

Cost of house............................... $140,000

Commission expense.................... 8,000 (= $800 + $7,200)

General expenses......................... 4,000

Total expenses....................... 152,000

Income..................................... $ 8,000

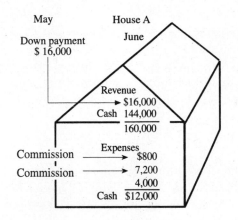

According to Exhibit 6.1, cash transactions in June were:

June	Event	Cash Increases	Cash Decreases
2	Down payment on House *B*	$ 24,000	
5	Final payment on House *A*	144,000	
30	Commission on House *B*		$1,200
	General expenses for June		4,000

In June, Cash increased by a net amount of $162,800. This increase had no relation to the $8,000 income for June.

THE INCOME STATEMENT

The amount added to Retained Earnings as a result of profitable operations during a period is the **income** of the period. An income statement explains how this income was earned. The income statement is also called a profit and loss, or earnings, statement. There is no standard format for an income statement. The lower portion of Exhibit 6.2 shows one common format.

The first item on this income statement is Sales Revenue, which is the amount of products (i.e., goods and services) sold or delivered to customers during the period.

The item on the second line is labeled Cost of Sales. It reports the cost of the goods or services whose revenue is reported on the first line. This is an example of the matching concept.

The difference between sales and cost of sales is called gross margin. Thus,

$$\text{Gross Margin} = \text{Sales Revenue} - \text{Cost of Sales}$$

Operating expenses are subtracted from gross margin, producing **income before taxes**. In accordance with the matching concept, these expenses include costs related to the current period and costs that do not benefit future periods (i.e., losses).

The next item on Exhibit 6.2, provision for income taxes, is shown separately because it is an especially important expense.

The final item (the bottom line) on an income statement is called **net income** (or **net loss**, if expenses are larger than revenues).

To arrive at net income, **dividends** are not subtracted from revenues. Dividends are not an expense. Dividends are a distribution of earnings to shareholders.

A PACKAGE OF ACCOUNTING REPORTS

An income statement is a summary of certain changes in Retained Earnings that have taken place during an accounting period. Also, an income statement reports certain changes in Retained Earnings that have taken place between two balance sheets.

Thus, a useful accounting "report package" consists of a balance sheet *at the beginning of* the accounting period, an income statement *for* the period, and a balance sheet *at the end of* the period.

Exhibit 6.2 shows a financial report package consisting of an income statement and two balance sheets. The exhibit shows that Retained

EXHIBIT 6.2

A "PACKAGE" OF ACCOUNTING REPORTS
(000 OMITTED)

GARSDEN COMPANY

Condensed Balance Sheet as of December 31, 19x2		Condensed Balance Sheet as of December 31, 19x3	
Assets		**Assets**	
Current assets	$22,651	Current assets	$24,062
Buildings and equipment	13,412	Buildings and equipment	14,981
Other assets	2,176	Other assets	3,207
Total Assets	$38,239	Total Assets	$42,250
Liabilities and Equity		**Liabilities and Equity**	
Liabilities	$12,343	Liabilities	$14,622
Equity:		Equity:	
Paid-in capital	12,256	Paid-in capital	12,256
Retained earnings	13,640	Retained earnings	15,372
Total Liabilities and Equity	$38,239	Total Liabilities and Equity	$42,250

Income Statement
For the Year 19x3

Sales Revenue	$75,478
Less cost of sales	52,227
Gross margin	23,251
Less operating expenses	10,785
Income before taxes	12,466
Provision for income taxes	6,344
Net income	$ 6,122

Statement of Retained Earnings

Retained earnings, 12/31/x2	$13,640
Add Net income, 19x3	6,122
	19,762
Less dividends	4,390
Retained earnings, 12/31/x3	$15,372

Earnings on December 31, 19x2, was $13,640,000. During 19x3 profitable operations resulted in net income of $6,122,000, which increased Retained Earnings by this amount. (Net income is the **bottom line** on the income statement.)

Retained Earnings was decreased by $4,390,000, representing a distribution to the shareholders in the form of dividends. As a result, the total Retained Earnings on December 31, 19x3, was $15,372,000 (= $13,640,000 + $6,122,000- $4,390,000).

Remember that dividends are a distribution of earnings to owners. Dividends are *not* an expense.

The "package" of required financial statements includes a Statement of Cash Flows. This statement is described in Part 10.

INCOME STATEMENT PERCENTAGES

In an analysis of a business's performance, **percentages** of certain income statement items are usually calculated. The base (i.e., 100 percent) is sales revenue. One percentage is the **gross margin percentage**, which is found by dividing gross margin by sales revenue.

The gross margin percentage for Garsden Company in 19x3 would be:

$$\frac{\text{Gross margin}}{\text{Sales revenue}} = \frac{\$23,251}{\$75,478} = 31\%$$

An even more important percentage is the **net income percentage**, which for Garsden Company is:

$$\frac{\text{Net income}}{\text{Sales revenue}} = \frac{\$6,122}{\$75,478} = 8\%$$

The net income of many American manufacturing corporations is roughly 5–10% of sales revenue, but there is a wide variation from company to company.

REVIEW OF BASIC CONCEPTS

The nine basic concepts described in this book are listed below. These concepts are not stated as such in the accounting literature, but most accountants would agree that they are the basic underpinnings of accounting.

Dual-aspect concept: Assets = Liabilities + Equity.

Money-measurement concept: Accounting reports only facts that can be expressed in monetary amounts.

Entity concept: Accounts are kept for an entity, as distinguished from the persons associated with that entity.

Going-concern concept: Accounting assumes that an entity will continue to operate indefinitely and that it is not about to be sold or liquidated.

Cost concept: Accounting focuses on the cost of non-monetary assets, rather than on their market value.

Conservatism concept: Revenues are recognized when they are reasonably certain. Expenses are recognized when they are reasonably possible.

Materiality concept: Disregard insignificant matters. Disclose all important matters.

Realization concept: Revenues are recognized when goods or services are delivered.

Matching concept: The expenses of a period are costs associated with the revenues or activities of the period.

KEY POINTS TO REMEMBER

- Expenditures are made when goods or services are acquired. If these goods or services are used up during the current period, they are expenses of the period. If not used up, they are assets at the end of that period. These assets will become expenses in future periods as they are used up.

- Some expenditures result in liabilities that will be paid in future periods. An example is accrued salaries.

- Expenses are expired costs. Assets are unexpired costs.

- Matching concept: Costs associated with the revenues or activities of a period are expenses of the period.

- Expenses of a period are (1) cost of the products (i.e., goods and services) that were delivered to customers during the period; (2) other expenditures that benefit operations of the period; and (3) losses, that is, decreases in assets from fire, theft, and other unusual reasons, and increases in liabilities from unusual events, such as lawsuits.

- The income statement summarizes revenues and expenses of the period. Its "bottom line," or net income, shows the increase in equity resulting from activities during the period.

- Dividends are a distribution of earnings to shareholders. Dividends are *not* expenses.

- Retained Earnings at the beginning of the period + Net Income – Dividends = Retained Earnings at the end of the period.

- Percentages are calculated for various income statement items, especially gross margin and net income, taking sales revenue as 100 percent.

PART 7

Inventories and Cost of Sales

This part describes:
* How the cost of sales is calculated.
* Methods of arriving at inventory amounts.
* When inventory amounts on the balance sheet are reduced.
* How inventory is measured in a manufacturing company.
* The distinction between product costs and period costs.
* How overhead rates are calculated.

FINDING COST OF SALES

In the income statement in Part 6, the first item subtracted from sales revenue was called **Cost of sales**. (Some businesses call this item **Cost of goods sold**.) It is the cost of the same products whose revenues are included in the sales amount. This is an example of the matching concept. In most businesses the cost of sales is the largest item of expense, amounting to as much as 85% of sales revenues in a profitable supermarket and 60–70% in a profitable manufacturing company.

In some entities, matching cost of sales and sales revenue is easy. For example, an automobile dealer keeps a record of the cost of each automobile in its inventory. If the dealer sold two automobiles during a given month, one for $18,000 that had cost $16,000, and the other for $10,000 that had cost $7,500, sales revenue for the period would be recorded as $28,000 and cost of sales as $23,500. This is the **specific identification** method.

> *Example.* A dealer sold an automobile costing $16,000 for $18,000 cash. The journal entry that records the effect of this transaction solely on the Sales Revenue and Cash accounts follows:

```
Dr. Cash....................  18,000
    Cr. Sales Revenue .........        18,000
```

> The journal entry to record the effect of this transaction solely upon the Inventory and Cost of Sales accounts is:

```
Dr. Cost of Sales............  16,000
    Cr. Inventory ............        16,000
```

A dealer that sells refrigerators might keep a record of its inventory of each type of refrigerator, something like the following:

Item: Refrigerator #602, Cost $200 each

Date	Receipts		Shipments to Customers		On Hand	
	Quantity	Cost	Quantity	Cost	Quantity	Cost
May 1					4	800
6			1	200	3	600
10	10	2,000			13	2,600
13			6	1,200	7	1,400
31			2	400	5	1,000
Totals	10	2,000	9	1,800	5	1,000

This is called a **perpetual inventory** record. "Receipts" are increases in inventory, and "Shipments to Customers" are decreases in inventory.

Information in the perpetual inventory records corresponds to that in the Inventory account. From the inventory record, we see that the beginning balance in the Inventory account for Refrigerator #602 on May 1 was $800. There were receipts during May of $2,000, which added to Inventory; these were a Dr. to the Inventory account. Shipments during May decreased inventory by $1,800, which were a Cr. to the Inventory account. This decrease in inventory was the Cost of Sales in May, which was $1,800.

Using the *totals* in the perpetual inventory record, the inventory transactions for May would be recorded in T-accounts as given below. (The inventory purchases were on credit.)

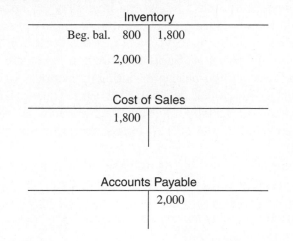

Refrigerators that cost $1,800 were sold in May for $2,500. The following partial income statement reflects this, assuming these were the only items sold.

Income Statement	
May	
Sales revenue	$2,500
Cost of sales	1,800
Gross margin	700

FINDING COST OF SALES BY DEDUCTION

If an entity has a perpetual inventory, as illustrated above, finding cost of sales in a month is easy. Thanks to computers, many more companies use the perpetual inventory method. We shall next show how to deduce cost of sales in a business that does not have this record. This method is the process of **deduction**.

Many stores, such as hardware stores, carry so many relatively low-value items that keeping a perpetual inventory record for each separate item is not practical. When the salesperson rings up a sale on the cash register, a record is made of the sales revenue but not the cost of sales. (In a computerized environment, the cash register—or point-of-sale terminal—records both sales revenue and the cost of sales.) If a hardware store does not keep a record of the cost of each item in inventory, it must deduce cost of sales by an indirect method.

Items in a hardware store's **beginning inventory** on January 1, 19x1 were available for sale during 19x1. Additional items **purchased** and placed on the shelves during 19x1 were also available for sale during 19x1. Therefore, the **goods available for sale** in a period are the sum of the beginning inventory plus purchases during the period.

For example, assume that on January 1, 19x1, Cantal Hardware had an inventory that cost $200,000. During 19x1 it purchased $600,000 of additional merchandise. The cost of **goods available for sale** in 19x1 was $800,000.

Accountants assume that goods available for sale during a period either were in inventory at the end of the period or they were sold. Thus, if goods costing $800,000 were available for sale during 19x1 and goods costing $300,000 were in inventory on December 31, 19x1, cost of sales in 19x1 is assumed to be $500,000.

At the end of each accounting period, all goods currently on hand are counted. This process is called **taking a physical inventory**. Since its purpose is to find the cost of the goods that were sold, each item is reported at its cost. In order to determine the ending inventory of one period and the beginning inventory of the next period, only one physical inventory must be taken, because the ending inventory on December 31, 19x1 is also the beginning inventory on January 1, 19x2.

"Cost of sales" and "Cost of goods sold" mean the same thing. We shall use the shorter term, **cost of sales**. In the deduction method for determining cost of sales, goods are assumed to have been sold if they are not in inventory at the end of the period.

Entities that use the perpetual inventory method take a physical inventory at least annually. This inventory may reveal that the actual ending inventory is lower than is indicated in the perpetual inventory records, because of theft, errors in record keeping, or items that have been damaged or discarded. If so, the ending inventory is reduced by a credit entry in order to record this **shrinkage**. The offsetting debit entry is to an expense account, Loss on Inventory.

Cost of sales can be found by subtracting the ending inventory from the total goods available, as in the following table:

Cost (000 omitted)	
Beginning inventory	$200
Purchases	600
Total goods available	800
Ending inventory	300
Cost of sales	500

The same situation is shown in the following diagram.

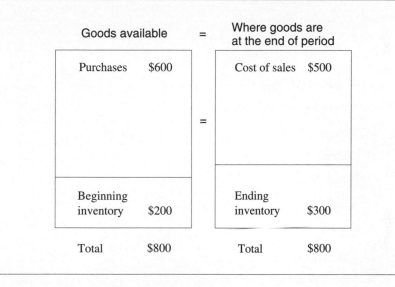

INVENTORY VALUATION ASSUMPTIONS

In the preceding example, we assumed that all units of a given item, such as all Refrigerator #602, were purchased at the same cost. Actually, the cost of goods purchased at different times may differ. For example, because inflation leads to increases in cost, the cost of goods purchased recently may be higher than the cost of the same goods purchased some time ago. In the following pages, we describe the three principal methods of finding cost of sales and ending inventory in such a situation.

Lewis Fuel Company deals in fuel oil. Its inventory and purchases during April are shown in Exhibit 7.1. The "Unit Cost" column shows that fuel oil entered the inventory at different unit costs during April.

EXHIBIT 7.1

LEWIS FUEL COMPANY

	Quantity	Unit Cost	Total Cost
Beginning inventory, April 1	400	1.00	400
Purchases, April 10	300	1.10	330
Purchases, April 20	300	1.20	360
Total goods available	1,000		1,090
Ending inventory, April 30	600		?
Cost of sales, April			?

FIFO METHOD

Goods available	$1,090

Ending inventory:

300 units @ $1.20 = ...	$360
300 units @ $1.10 = ...	330
Total 600 units	690
Cost of sales	$ 400

LIFO METHOD

Goods available	$1,090

Ending inventory:

400 units @ $1.00 = ...	$400
200 units @ $1.10=	220
Total 600 units	620
Cost of sales	$ 470

AVERAGE-COST METHOD

Average cost of

$$\frac{\$1,090}{1,000} = \$1.09 \text{ cost per unit}$$

Goods available	$1,090
Ending inventory: 600 units @ $1.09 = ...	$654
Cost of sales: 400 units @ $1.09 =..............	$436

The problem is: What unit cost should we assign to the ending inventory? There are three choices: (1) we could assume that the older fuel oil was sold, leaving the newer fuel oil in inventory; (2) we could assume that the newer fuel oil was sold, leaving the older fuel in inventory; or (3) we could assume that a mixture of old and new oil was sold.

Because the fuel oil has been mixed together in the storage tank, we do not have a record of the cost of the specific quantities of fuel oil actually sold during the month. Therefore the solution is not clearcut.

First-In, First-Out (FIFO) Method

In this situation, many companies make the First-In, First-Out (FIFO) assumption. They assume that the goods that came into the inventory first are the first to move out.

In the FIFO method, we assume that the older fuel oil was sold during the month and that the newer fuel oil remains in the ending inventory. Therefore, in Exhibit 7.1, the ending inventory of 600 units of fuel oil is assumed to be the most recently purchased fuel oil—namely, the 300 units that were purchased on April 20 at $1.20 per unit, and the 300 units purchased on April 10 at $1.10 per unit.

The ending inventory under the FIFO method therefore is:

$$
\begin{array}{ll}
300 \text{ units @ } \$1.20 = \$360 \\
\underline{300 \text{ units @ } \$1.10 = \$330} \\
600 \text{ units} \qquad\qquad \$690
\end{array}
$$

The cost of goods available for sale was $1,090. We enter this amount in our calculation and subtract the ending inventory of $690 from it. The difference is the FIFO cost of sales, which is $400.

Last-In, First-Out (LIFO) Method

The FIFO method assumes that the oldest units, those First In, were the first to be sold, that is, they were the First Out. The LIFO method assumes the opposite, namely, that the newest units, which were the Last In, were the first to be sold, that is, they were First Out, hence the name Last-In, First-Out.

Because the LIFO method assumes that the last units purchased were the first ones to be sold, the ending inventory is assumed to consist of any remaining units in beginning inventory, plus the earliest units purchased. In Exhibit 7.1, the ending inventory was 600 units, and in the LIFO method these 600 units are assumed to be the 400 units in beginning inventory plus 200 of the 300 units purchased on April 10.

Under the LIFO method, the amount available for sale remains $1,090; the ending inventory is

$$
\begin{array}{ll}
400 \text{ units @ } \$1.00 = \$400 \\
\underline{200 \text{ units @ } \$1.10 = \$220} \\
600 \text{ units} \qquad\qquad \$620
\end{array}
$$

and the cost of sales is $1,090 - $620 = $470.

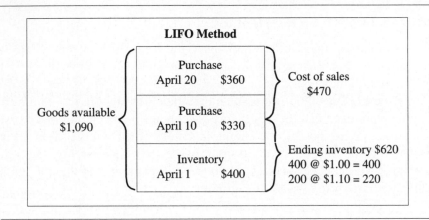

Average-Cost Method

The third method is the **average-cost method**. It calculates the cost of both the ending inventory and the cost of sales at the average cost per unit of the goods available. In Exhibit 7.1, the number of units available in April was 1,000, and the total cost of these goods was $1,090, so the average cost per unit was $1.09.

Using the average cost of $1.09 per unit, the ending inventory is
600 units @ $1.09 = $654.

Cost of Sales is therefore
400 units @ $1.09 = $436.

Comparison of Inventory Methods

Most businesses try to sell their oldest goods first, so the goods that were first in are likely to be the goods first out. The FIFO method reflects this practice.

From Exhibit 7.1, we see that cost of sales under FIFO was $400 and under LIFO it was $470. Cost of sales was higher under LIFO.

In most companies, in periods of rising prices (i.e., inflation) this same relationship holds; that is, cost of sales is higher under LIFO than under FIFO.

In calculating income taxes, cost of sales is one of the items subtracted from revenue in order to find taxable income. Assume the revenue of Lewis Fuel Company was $1,000. Disregarding other expenses, if cost of sales was $470, taxable income would be $530. If cost of sales was $400, taxable income would be $600, which is $70 higher.

Thus, the higher the cost of sales, the lower the taxable income. The lower the taxable income, the lower the income tax based on that income will be.

Companies usually prefer to pay as low an income tax as they legally can. Therefore, they prefer the method that results in the higher cost of sales. If prices are rising, this is usually the LIFO method.

Any of the methods described above is permitted in calculating taxable income in the United States. However, a company cannot switch back and forth between methods from one year to the next. In many countries, the LIFO method is not permitted.

INVENTORY VALUATION: ADJUSTMENT TO MARKET

We have assumed so far that inventory is recorded at its cost. Suppose, however, that the market value of the inventory falls below its original cost. The conservatism concept requires that we reduce the inventory to the lower amount.

For this reason, if the market value of an item of inventory at the end of an accounting period is lower than its original cost, the item is "written down" to its market value. For example, an item whose original cost was $100 and whose current market value is $80 should be written down by $20. This is an exception to the general rule that nonmonetary assets are reported at cost. This rule is called **LOCOM**, which is the abbreviation for "lower of cost or market."

In "writing down" inventory, the Inventory account is credited, and Cost of Sales is debited.

Example. If inventory is written down by $20, the appropriate journal entry would be:

```
Dr. Cost of Sales...........     20
    Cr. Inventory ............            20
```

INVENTORY IN A MANUFACTURING COMPANY

A company that sells finished goods that it purchased from other companies to customers is a merchandising company. A company that converts raw materials into finished goods and then sells these goods is a manufacturing company. Retail stores, wholesalers, and distributors are merchandising companies. A company that makes shoes is a manufacturing company.

A merchandising company buys its goods in salable form and receives an invoice showing the cost for each item. The costs on these invoices are the amounts used to record the additions to inventory. A manufacturing company adds value to the raw material it buys; it must include these **conversion costs** in its inventory and in its cost of sales. Measuring inventory and cost of sales therefore is more complicated in a manufacturing company.

In a **manufacturing** company, the cost of a finished product consists of three elements:

- cost of **materials** used directly in that product;

- cost of **labor** used directly on that product; and

- a fair share of **overhead** costs associated with the production process.

Some materials, such as oil for lubricating machinery, are not used directly on a product. The materials that are used directly in the product are called direct materials. Similarly, the labor used directly to make the product is called direct labor.

Production overhead consists of all other production costs; that is, production costs that are not direct materials or direct labor. In some manufacturing companies, computers and automated machine tools replace workers, so direct labor cost is relatively small. These companies combine labor costs and production overhead costs into a single item called **Other Production Costs**.

The three elements of production cost—**direct labor**, **direct materials**, and **overhead**—are added together to determine the total cost of the finished product. Until the product is sold, this amount is held in inventory. When the product is sold, this amount becomes Cost of Sales. Thus, if a product requires $5 of direct labor, $7 of direct materials, and $3 of overhead, the product will be costed at $15 as long as it is in the Inventory account. When it is sold, Cost of Sales will be $15.

The process of assigning production costs to products is called **cost accounting**. The assignment of costs to various services in banks, schools, hotels, and all types of service organizations also involves cost accounting. We shall describe some of its major aspects.

Product Costs and Period Costs

Costs are divided into two categories, which are treated differently for purposes of accounting:

- **product costs**—those that are associated with the production of products, and

- **period costs**—those that are associated with the sales and general activities of the accounting period.

For example, the cost of heating the offices of the sales department would be considered a period cost. The cost of heating the production plant itself would be a product cost.

It is relatively easy to keep track of direct labor and the direct materials costs. The measurement of overhead costs is more complicated.

Overhead costs that are classified as product costs are added to direct labor costs and direct material costs in order to find the amount at which the products are costed in the Inventory account. If, during 19x1, Jones Manufacturing Company spent $10,000 on production overhead, $100,000 on direct labor and $20,000 on direct materials, and if no products were sold, its Inventory item on the December 31, 19x1, balance sheet will increase by $130,000. If these products (and no others) were sold in 19x2, Cost of Sales in 19x2 will be $130,000.

Product costs do not affect income until the product is sold. At that time, product costs become Cost of Sales. Thus, if $10,000 of overhead is counted as a product cost in 19x1, and if the goods with which these product costs were associated are sold in 19x2, the $10,000 of overhead costs will appear as a part of Cost of Sales in 19x2.

By contrast, costs that are classified as **period** costs are treated as part of the operating expenses of the period in which they are incurred. For example, if 19x1 period costs in Jones Manufacturing Company were $50,000, the $50,000 of period costs would be an expense in 19x1, even if the products produced in 19x1 were not sold until 19x2.

> *Example.* Suppose that in January the total overhead costs in Lee Shoe Company were $100,000, and that 40% of this overhead was associated with the production activities of the business and 60% with the sales and general activities. The amount of overhead that is a product cost therefore is $40,000, and the amount that is a period cost is $60,000.
>
> Since Lee Shoe Company recognized $60,000 as a period cost for January, this $60,000 will be charged as an expense in January. (The word "charged" means "debited.")
>
> Suppose the shoes manufactured in January are sold in February. The $40,000 of product overhead costs will be included in Inventory at the end of January and will be part of Cost of Sales in February.

Period costs reduce income in the period in which the costs are incurred. Product costs reduce income in the period in which the products are sold, which is often a later period.

Overhead Rates

Another overhead problem is how to divide the total product overhead cost among the various products produced. For example, it is hard to say how much of the cost of heating a shoe factory should be charged to each pair of shoes made in the factory. Any of several methods may be used to charge overhead costs to various products. Usually these methods make use of an overhead rate.

> **Example.** Lee Shoe Company incurred $40,000 of production overhead costs during January. If 5,000 hours of direct labor were used during January, then $8 (= $40,000 ÷ 5,000 hours) of overhead cost might be charged for each hour of direct labor. This amount per hour is the overhead rate. If a certain pair of shoes requires 1/2 hour of direct labor, and if the overhead rate is $8 per direct labor hour, the amount of overhead cost charged to those shoes would be $4.
>
> Suppose the direct materials used in a certain pair of shoes cost $10. One-half hour of direct labor at $12 per hour was also used. The overhead rate is $8 per direct labor hour. The cost of the shoes is recorded at $20 [= $10 + (.5 * $12) + (.5 * $8)].

There are many other types of overhead rates: a rate per machine hour, a rate per labor dollar, or a rate per material dollar. Whatever the rate, its purpose is to assign a fair share of overhead cost to each product.

INVENTORY TURNOVER

In earlier parts we described ratios and percentages that are useful in analyzing financial statements. For example, the gross margin percentage is a ratio of

$$\frac{\textbf{Gross Margin}}{\textbf{Sales Revenue}}$$

A useful ratio for analyzing inventory is the **inventory turnover ratio**. This ratio shows how many *times* the inventory turned over during a year. It is found by dividing Cost of Sales for a period by Inventory at the end of the period (or by the average inventory during the period).

> **Example.** Cost of Sales for 19x1 was $1,000,000. Inventory on December 31, 19x1, was $200,000. The inventory turnover ratio, showing how many times the inventory turned over in 19x1, was

$$\frac{\text{Cost of Sales}}{\text{Inventory}} = \frac{\$1,000,000}{\$200,000} = 5 \text{ times}$$

Slow-moving inventory ties up capital and increases the risk that the goods will become obsolete. Thus, an inventory turnover of five times is generally better than an inventory turnover of four times. However, if inventory is too small, orders from customers may not be filled promptly, which can result in lost sales revenue. This would reduce both cash and income.

Look back at the calculation of the inventory turnover ratio. The turnover ratio can be increased either by selling more goods with the same level of inventory or by having less inventory for the same amount of sales volume.

KEY POINTS TO REMEMBER

- If an entity has no record of the cost of the specific items that were sold during a period, it deduces Cost of Sales by (1) adding purchases to the beginning inventory, which gives the goods available for sale, and (2) subtracting the cost of the ending Inventory.

- In doing this, it must make an assumption as to which items were sold.

- The First-In, First-Out (FIFO) method assumes that the oldest items are the first to be sold.

- The Last-In, First-Out (LIFO) method assumes that the most recently purchased items are the first to be sold. In periods of rising prices, it results in a higher Cost of Sales and hence a lower taxable income than the FIFO method.

- The average-cost method costs both Cost of Sales and the ending Inventory at the average cost of the goods available for sale.

- The inventory method that a company selects does not necessarily reflect the physical flow of its goods.

- If the market value of items in inventory decreases below their cost, the inventory is written down to cost.

- The cost of goods produced in a manufacturing company is the sum of their direct materials cost, direct labor cost, and production overhead cost.

- Period costs are those that are charged as expenses in the period in which the costs were incurred.

- Product costs become Cost of Sales in the period in which the products are sold, which may be later than the period in which the products were manufactured.

- Overhead is charged to products by means of an overhead rate, such as a rate per direct labor hour.

- The inventory turnover ratio shows how many times the inventory turned over during a year.

PART 8

Noncurrent Assets and Depreciation

This part describes:
*   How plant assets are recorded in the accounts.
*   The meaning and significance of depreciation.
*   Straight-line, accelerated, and units-of-production methods of depreciation.
*   How depreciation is recorded.
*   Differences between income-tax principles and accounting principles.
*   The meaning of depletion and how it is recorded.
*   How intangible assets are recorded.

NONCURRENT ASSETS

Earlier, we learned that current assets are cash or items likely to be converted to cash within one year. **Noncurrent assets** are expected to be of use to the entity for longer than one year.

Tangible assets are assets that can be touched. **Intangible assets** are assets that have no physical substance (other than as pieces of paper) but give the entity valuable rights.

On the balance sheet, tangible noncurrent assets are often labeled **fixed assets**, or **property, plant, and equipment**. Equipment is a noncurrent, tangible asset. For brevity, we shall use the word **plant** for all tangible noncurrent assets except land. Thus, buildings, equipment, and furniture are items of plant. These assets are expected to be useful for longer than one year.

ACCOUNTING FOR ACQUISITIONS

When an item of plant is acquired, it is recorded in the accounts at its cost in accordance with the fundamental accounting concept known as the **cost concept**.

The cost of an asset includes all costs incurred to make the asset ready for its intended use.

> *Example.* Bird Corporation paid $50,000 for a plot of land. It also paid $1,500 as a broker's fee, $600 for legal fees, and $5,000 to tear down the existing structures in order to make the land ready for a new building. The land should be recorded in the accounts at an amount of $57,100. (Some accountants charge the $5,000 as a cost of the new building.)

Transportation and installation costs are usually included as part of equipment cost. For example, assume that Plymouth Bank purchased a computer for $40,000, and that the bank also paid $200 in freight charges and $1,000 in installation charges. This equipment should be recorded in the accounts at its cost, $41,200.

If an entity constructs a machine or a building with its own personnel, all costs incurred in construction are included in the asset amount.

> *Example.* Thayer Company built a new building for its own use. It spent $200,000 in materials, $900,000 in compensation to workers directly engaged in the building's construction, and $200,000 in overhead costs related to the building. This building should be recorded in the accounts at its cost, $1,300,000.

CAPITAL LEASES

Most assets are *owned* by the entity. When an entity **leases** (i.e., rents) a building, a machine, or other tangible item, the item is owned by someone else (the **lessor**); the entity does not own it. Therefore, most leased items are not assets of the entity that leases them (the **lessee**).

However, if an entity leases an item for a long period of time, it has as much control over the use of that item as if it owned it. A lease for a long time—almost the whole life of the asset—is called a **capital lease**. Because the entity controls the item for almost its whole life, a capital lease is recorded as an asset.

The amount recorded for a capital lease is the amount the entity would have paid if it had purchased the item rather than leased it. If an entity leased a machine for 10 years, agreeing to pay $10,000 per year, and if the purchase price of this machine was $70,000, this capital lease would be recorded as an asset at an amount of $70,000, as in this entry:

```
Dr. Capital lease...........   70,000
    Cr. Lease obligation ......          70,000
```

Even though the entity does not own the item, a capital lease is treated like other plant assets. A capital lease is an exception to the general rule that assets are property or property rights that are owned by the entity. Special rules apply to accounting for capital leases. They are beyond the scope of this introductory treatment.

DEPRECIATION

Except in rare cases, **land** retains its usefulness indefinitely. Land therefore continues to be reported on the balance sheet at its acquisition cost, in accordance with the cost concept. If Hanover Hospital purchased a plot of land in 1970 at a cost of $100,000, it would have been reported at $100,000 on the December 31, 1970, balance sheet. If Hanover Hospital still owned the land in 1996, and its market value then was $300,000, it would be reported on the December 31, 1996, balance sheet at $100,000.

Unlike land, a plant asset eventually becomes useless; that is, it has a limited life. At the end of its life, when it becomes completely useless, the item is no longer an asset. Usually this process occurs gradually; that is, a portion of the asset is used up in each year of its life, until finally it is scrapped or sold and therefore is no longer useful to the entity.

The period of time over which a plant asset is estimated to be of **service** to the company is called its **service life**. When a machine or other item of plant is acquired, we do not know how long it actually will be of service. Therefore, we must estimate its service life.

Since some portion of a plant asset is used up during each year of its service life, a portion of the cost of the asset is treated as an expense in each year. For example, suppose a computer is purchased at a cost of $50,000. It has an estimated service life of five years and will be worthless then. It would be reasonable to charge one fifth, or $10,000, as expense in each of the five years.

The process of recognizing a portion of the cost of a plant asset as an expense during each year of its estimated service life is called **depreciation**. The $10,000 recorded as an expense during each one of the five years of service life of the computer that cost $50,000 is called the **depreciation expense** for that year.

A plant asset can become useless for either of two reasons: (1) it may wear out physically; or (2) it may become obsolete. The latter reason is called **obsolescence**. Loss of usefulness because of the development of improved equipment, changes in style, or other causes not related to the physical condition of the asset are examples of obsolescence.

The **service life** of an asset considers both physical wear and obsolescence. The service life is the shorter of the two periods. Thus an asset with an estimated physical life of ten years that is estimated to become obsolete in five years has an estimated service life of five years.

Since depreciation considers obsolescence, it is not correct to regard depreciation and obsolescence as two different things.

To summarize:

- Depreciation is the process of converting the cost of an asset into expense over its service life.

- This process recognizes that an asset gradually loses its usefulness.

- An asset can lose its usefulness for either of two reasons:

    - it wears out, or

    - it becomes obsolete.

- The asset's service life is the shorter of these two causes.

In the summary above, no mention was made of market value. Depreciation is not related to changes in the market value of an asset. This is consistent with the cost concept.

In some cases, an entity expects to be able to sell the plant asset at the end of its service life. The amount that it expects to sell it for is called its **residual value**. For example, if an entity buys a truck for $20,000 and expects to sell it for $4,000 five years later, the estimated residual value is $4,000. In most cases, an entity expects that a plant asset will be worthless at the end of its service life. If so, its residual value is zero.

Note that residual value, as such, does not appear in the accounts.

Example. Suppose a restaurant oven that cost $22,000 is expected to have a residual value of $2,000 at the end of its 10-year life. In this case, the total amount of depreciation that should be recorded during the service life of the asset is only $20,000. The depreciation expense for each of the ten years would be $2,000 (= $20,000 * 1/10).

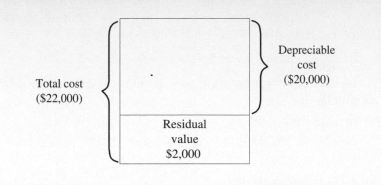

The difference between the cost of a plant asset and its residual value is called the **depreciable cost**. Thus, if an automobile purchased for $10,000 is expected to have a six-year life, and to have a residual value of $1,000 at the end of that life, $10,000 is the cost (or gross cost) and $9,000 is the depreciable cost.

Here is a list of factors that are relevant to the depreciation of an asset:

1. Original cost;

2. Residual value; and

3. Service life.

We use (1) and (2) to arrive at depreciable cost. All three factors are used to calculate depreciation expense for a given year. Note that factors (2) and (3) are estimates.

DEPRECIATION METHODS

There are many methods of calculating the cost that is to be recorded as depreciation expense in each year of the estimated service life. In the following sections we describe three of them:

1. Units-of-production depreciation;

2. Straight-line depreciation; and

3. Accelerated depreciation.

Units-of-Production Depreciation

In the units-of-production method, a cost per unit of production is calculated, and depreciation expense for a year is found by multiplying this unit cost by the number of units that the asset produced in that year.

Example. Grady Company purchased a truck in 19x1 for $44,000. It estimated that the truck would provide services for 100,000 miles and would have a residual value of $4,000.

Its depreciable cost was $40,000 (= $44,000 – $4,000).

Its estimated cost per mile was $0.40 (= $40,000 ÷ 100,000 miles).

In 19x2, the truck was driven 15,000 miles. Its depreciation expense in 19x2 was $6,000 (= $0.40 * 15,000 miles).

Straight-Line Depreciation

The depreciation of a plant asset with a cost of $10,000, no residual value, and a five-year life may be graphed as follows:

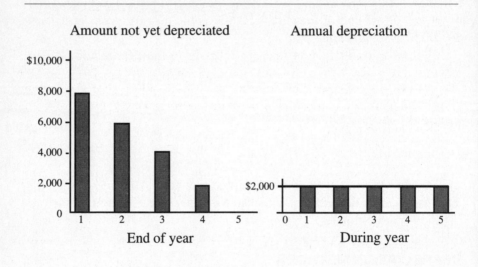

The line showing depreciation expense as a function of time is a straight line. Because of this, charging off an equal fraction of the asset cost each year is called the straight-line method of depreciation. Most companies use this method.

The percentage of cost charged off each year is called the **depreciation rate**. In the straight-line method, we obtain the rate by finding:

$$\frac{1}{\text{number of years of service life}}$$

Examples.

If the estimated life of an asset is:	The straight-line depreciation rate is:
2 years	50%
3 years	33-1/3%
4 years	25%
5 years	20%

In the straight-line method, the amount of depreciation expense for a given year is found by multiplying the depreciable cost by the depreciation rate. Thus, if the depreciable cost is $9,000 and the depreciation rate is 20%, the amount of depreciation expense each year will be $1,800.

Accelerated Depreciation

If you want an automobile to go faster, you press down on the accelerator. **Accelerated Depreciation** writes off the cost of an asset faster than straight-line depreciation. In accelerated depreciation, more depreciation expense is reported in the early years of the asset's service life and therefore less in the later years. The total amount of depreciation expense is the same as in the straight-line method.

There are many ways of calculating accelerated depreciation amounts. The following table shows one of them. The asset has a depreciable cost of $15,000 and a service life of five years.

Year	Accelerated Depreciation	Straight-line Depreciation	Accelerated is
1	$5,000	$3,000	larger
2	4,000	3,000	larger
3	3,000	3,000	same
4	2,000	3,000	smaller
5	1,000	3,000	smaller
Total	15,000	15,000	same

Accelerated depreciation is used principally in calculating taxable income, as we shall see in a later section.

ACCOUNTING FOR DEPRECIATION

In Part 6 we described how certain types of assets were converted into expenses with the passage of time. When this occurs, there is a Cr. entry to the asset account, which shows the decrease in the amount of the asset, and there is an equal Dr. to the expense account.

> *Example.* If an entity had a fuel oil asset of $2,000 at the beginning of March and used $500 of fuel oil during March, the entity will recognize $500 of fuel oil expense for March, and it will also recognize an equal decrease of $500 in the fuel oil asset. On the balance sheet of March 31, the fuel oil asset will be reported at $1,500.

In accounting for depreciation, the procedure is similar. First, we recognize the appropriate amount of expense for the period. In this case the title of the expense account is Depreciation Expense.

Next, we recognize an equal decrease in the amount of the asset. However, accountants prefer to show the original cost of plant assets on the balance sheet at all times. Therefore, decreases in the amount of a plant asset are not shown as a direct reduction in the asset amount. Instead, decreases in the asset amount of a plant asset because of depreciation expense are accumulated in a separate account called **Accumulated Depreciation**.

A decrease in an asset is always a credit. Accumulated Depreciation is a decrease in an asset and therefore has a Cr. balance. Accumulated Depreciation is a **contra-asset** account.

If $1,000 of depreciation expense is recognized for a given year, the appropriate journal entry would be:

```
Dr. Depreciation Expense ......  1,000
    Cr. Accumulated Depreciation          1,000
```

On the balance sheet, the balance in the Accumulated Depreciation account is shown as a deduction from the original cost of the asset, and the remaining amount is called **book value**. For example, the listing:

Plant	$10,000
Less accumulated depreciation	4,000
Book value	$ 6,000

shows that the plant originally cost $10,000, that $4,000 of its original cost has so far been recognized as depreciation expense, and that $6,000 of book value remains to be depreciated in future years. (Part of the book value may be the estimated residual value.)

If the depreciation expense on this machine was $1,000 per year, we know from the above that depreciation expense has been taken for four years, and that it will be taken for six more years in the future, assuming zero residual value. Each year, the write- off of $1,000 of the cost of the asset would be recorded with the following journal entry:

```
Dr. Depreciation Expense ...... 1,000
    Cr. Accumulated Depreciation          1,000
```

The table below shows the original cost, annual depreciation expense, accumulated depreciation (at year end), and book value (at year end) for a plant asset with an original cost of $5,000, a service life of five years, and zero residual value.

Year	Original Cost	Depreciation Expense	Accumulated Depreciation	Book Value
19x1	$5,000	$1,000	$1,000	$4,000
19x2	5,000	1,000	2,000	3,000
19x3	5,000	1,000	3,000	2,000
19x4	5,000	1,000	4,000	1,000
19x5	5,000	1,000	5,000	zero

The total amount charged as depreciation expense during the service life of the asset is thus $5,000.

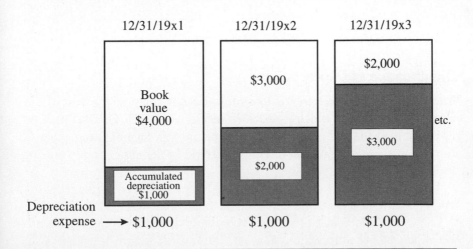

At the end of 19x3, for example, the asset would be reported on the company's balance sheet as

Plant	$5,000
Less accumulated depreciation	3,000
Book value	$2,000

After the cost of an asset has been completely written off as depreciation expense, no more depreciation is recorded, even though the asset continues to be used. In the example given above, the book value at the end of 19x5 is zero. If the asset continued to be used in 19x6, depreciation expense in 19x6 would be zero.

Sale of a Plant Asset

The calculation of book value depends on estimates of service life and residual value. Because the actual residual value may differ from these estimates, the amount realized from the sale of a plant asset will probably be different from its book value. (Hence, book value does not report the market value of the asset.) The difference between book value and the amount actually realized from a sale of a plant asset is called a **gain** (or **loss**) **on disposition of plant**. For example, if an asset whose book value is $10,000 is sold for $12,000, $2,000 would be the gain on disposition of plant and would be so reported on the income statement.

When the asset is sold, its cost and its accumulated depreciation are removed from the accounts. For an asset that cost $40,000, had accumulated depreciation of $30,000, and sold for $12,000, the journal entry would be:

```
Cash ......................... 12,000
Accumulated Depreciation ...... 30,000
     Plant ....................           40,000
        Gain on disposition of plant       2,000
```

Significance of Depreciation

The purpose of depreciation is to write off a fair share of the cost of the asset in each year in which it provides service. Actually, an asset may be as valuable at the end of a year as at the beginning. Depreciation expense for a given year does not represent a decrease in the asset's real value or usefulness during the year.

Also, don't forget that in accounting for plant assets, original cost is known, but both service life and residual value are estimates.

The book value of a plant asset represents that portion of the cost not yet expensed. Therefore the statement "book value reports what the asset is worth" is incorrect.

DEPRECIATION FOR INCOME TAX PURPOSES

Corporations and individuals are subject to a tax on their income. The **income tax** is calculated as a percentage of taxable income. If a corporation has taxable income of $1 million, and if the income tax rate is 40%, the corporation would pay an income tax of $400,000.

Income tax rates are set on a sliding scale; the rates are higher for higher levels of income. In this book, we use a flat rate of 40% in order to avoid the additional arithmetic that would be necessary with the actual sliding scale. Also, the 40% rate is rounded upward from the highest U.S. corporate tax rate.

The Internal Revenue Service publishes regulations explaining how to calculate **taxable income**. We shall refer to these regulations as **tax accounting principles**. Most tax accounting principles are consistent with financial accounting principles, but some are not. As a result, taxable income and **financial accounting income** may differ. When a choice is possible, a business usually chooses the tax accounting principle that results in the lower taxable income.

In its accounting income statement, a business tries to report its income as *fairly* as possible. In determining the taxes it owes, a business tries to show a taxable income that is as *low* as legally possible. These two objectives are not the same.

For income tax purposes, depreciation is usually calculated according to what is called the **Modified Accelerated Cost Recovery System**. As the name suggests, the MACRS is an accelerated system.

In the MACRS, items of plant are assigned to one of six **recovery periods**, depending on their service lives. A schedule for each recovery period shows the percentage of cost that can be taken as depreciation expense in each year of the period. For example, for the seven-year recovery period, 69% of cost can be depreciated in the first half of the recovery period, and 31% in the second half. This contrasts with straight-line depreciation in which 50% of the cost is depreciated in the first half of the asset's life and 50% in the second half.

Also, assets classified in a certain recovery period typically have a longer service life than the life for which that recovery period is named. For example, many machinery and equipment items are classified in the seven-year recovery period, but their actual service life is typically longer than seven years.

MACRS depreciation results in a higher depreciation expense for tax purposes in the early years of an asset's life. This produces lower taxable income and lower income taxes during those early years.

In the later years of the asset's life, the MACRS system results in lower depreciation expense for tax purposes and higher taxable income and income taxes. The higher taxable income in later years will offset the lower taxable income in earlier years. However, during the earlier years the company has the use of the money not paid out in taxes. For this reason, most companies use MACRS depreciation for calculating taxable income, rather than the straight-line method. The government permits MACRS depreciation because it wants to encourage businesses to invest in new plant and equipment.

Taxable income and accounting income may differ. The tax regulations do not govern the way financial statements are prepared. Conversely, the way income is reported on a financial statement does not govern the way income is reported for tax purposes. There is one important exception to this: If LIFO is used in tax accounting, LIFO must also be used on the financial statements.

Deferred Income Taxes

If a company uses MACRS depreciation in calculating its taxable income but uses straight-line depreciation in calculating its accounting income, its taxable income in the early years will be lower than its accounting income, and its income tax will be correspondingly lower.

Example. Manley Corporation has accounting income in 19x1 of $2,000,000 but taxable income of only $1,500,000. If the income tax rate is 40%, it will pay an income tax of $600,000. If the income tax had been calculated as 40% of its accounting income, the amount of tax would have been $800,000.

Manley Corporation's actual tax payment of $600,000 is lower than the tax would be if it were calculated on its accounting income. The $600,000 does not match the accounting income. It is not consistent with the matching concept.

As required by the matching concept, the amount of income tax expense reported on the income statement is the amount of income tax calculated on the basis of accounting income, not the amount actually paid. Thus, if its accounting income was $2,000,000 and its tax rate 40 percent, Manley Corporation would report income tax expense of $800,000. If it actually paid only $600,000 income tax, it would somehow have to account for the difference of $200,000.

The difference between actual income taxes paid and income tax expense is called **Deferred Income Taxes**. It is a liability account on the balance sheet. Refer to Exhibit 1.1 on page 2. Garsden Company reported deferred income taxes as a noncurrent liability of $824,000. This is not to be confused with the **Estimated Tax Liability**, which is a current liability of $1,541,000. The latter amount is the amount it actually owed the government as of December 31, 1995, for its 1995 taxes.

Under certain circumstances, not described here, a company may have a deferred tax asset. It comes about when its taxable income is greater than its financial accounting income.

For example, if a company downsizes by promising a separation bonus to employees who agree to retire early, the cost of the bonus is an expense in the year in which the decision to downsize is made, but it is not a decrease in taxable income until the year in which the bonus is paid. Accounting income will therefore be lower than taxable income in the year the decision to downsize is made.

DEPLETION

Natural resources such as coal, oil, and other minerals are called **wasting assets**.

When the supply of oil in a well or coal in a mine is reduced, the asset is said to be depleted. **Depletion** is the name for the process of writing off the cost of wasting assets. The depletion of a wasting asset is similar to the depreciation of a plant asset. However, in accounting for depletion, the asset account is reduced directly. Therefore an accumulated depletion account is not ordinarily used.

Depletion is usually calculated by multiplying the quantity of the resource used in a period by a unit cost.

> *Example.* In 19x1 Cecil Company purchased a coal mine for $3,000,000. If it estimated that the mine contained 1,000,000 tons of coal, it would use a unit cost of $3 per ton.
>
> In 19x2, Cecil Company mined 100,000 tons of coal. Since the cost of this coal was estimated to be $3 per ton, the depletion expense in 19x2 was $300,000. The coal mine asset would appear on the balance sheet for December 31, 19x2 as:
>
> Coal mine $2,700,000

INTANGIBLE ASSETS

In accordance with the cost concept, intangible items such as goodwill, trademarks, and patents are not treated as assets unless they have been acquired at a measurable cost.

When intangibles are recognized as assets, their cost is written off over their service life. For example, patents have a maximum life of 17 years. In no case can the life of an intangible asset exceed 40 years. The process of writing off the cost of intangible assets is called **amortization**.

In summary, three terms that refer to writing off an asset's cost are:

1. **depreciation**, which refers to **plant** assets;
2. **depletion**, which refers to **wasting** assets; and
3. **amortization**, which refers to **intangible** assets.

Although we have used the word **amortization** just for intangible assets, amortization is sometimes used as a general term for expensing the cost of all assets; that is, some people call **depreciation** and **depletion** special cases of amortization.

KEY POINTS TO REMEMBER

- When acquired, a plant asset is recorded at its cost, including installation and other costs of making the asset ready for its intended use.

- Land has an unlimited life and is rarely depreciated.

- Plant assets are depreciated over their service life. Each year, a fraction of their cost is debited to Depreciation Expense and credited to Accumulated Depreciation.

- Depreciation Expense is an estimate. We do not know how long the service life will be, nor do we know the asset's residual value for certain.

- The book value of a plant asset is the difference between its cost and its accumulated depreciation. When book value reaches zero or the residual value, no more depreciation expense is recorded.

- Book value does not report what the asset is worth.

- When an asset is sold, the difference between the sales price and book value is a gain or loss and is so reported on the income statement.

- In financial accounting, depreciation is usually calculated either by the units-of-production method or by the straight-line method.

- In the units-of-production method, the annual depreciation expense is calculated by multiplying the number of service units produced in that year by a unit cost. This unit cost is found by dividing the asset's depreciable cost by the number of service units estimated to be produced over the asset's total life.

- In the straight-line method, the annual depreciation expense is calculated by multiplying the asset's depreciable cost by a constant percentage. This percentage is found by dividing 1 by the number of years in the asset's estimated service life. Most companies use the straight-line method.

- Accelerated depreciation is often used for income tax purposes because it decreases the amount of taxable income in the early years. The method used is called the Modified Accelerated Cost Recovery System (MACRS).

- Taxable income may differ from pretax income reported on the income statement. If so, the reported income tax expense is calculated on the basis of accounting pretax income. The difference between this amount and the amount of tax paid is a balance sheet item, Deferred Income Taxes.

- Depletion is the process of writing off wasting assets. Amortization is the process of writing off intangible assets. The accounting for both processes is similar to accounting for depreciation, except that the credit is made directly to the asset account.

PART 9

Liabilities and Equity

This part describes:
- The nature of working capital.
- Types of permanent capital: debt and equity.
- How to account for debt capital.
- Accounting for equity capital in proprietorships, partnerships, and corporations.
  - Paid-in capital: common and preferred stock.
  - Retained earnings and dividends.
- The debt/equity ratio.
- The nature of consolidated financial statements.

WORKING CAPITAL

The balance sheet has two sides with equal totals, as shown below.

LOUGEE COMPANY
Balance Sheet as of December 31, 19x1

Assets		Liabilities and Equity	
Current assets............................	$10,000	Current liabilities	$4,000
Noncurrent assets.....................	20,000	Noncurrent liabilities................	9,000
		Paid-in capital	7,000
		Retained earnings	10,000
Total assets	$30,000	Total liabilities and equity......	$30,000

Current assets are assets that are expected to be turned into cash within one year. Current liabilities are obligations that come due within one year. For Lougee Company, we can say that $4,000 of the $10,000 in current assets was financed by the current liabilities. The remaining $6,000 of current assets and the $20,000 of noncurrent assets were financed by the $9,000 of noncurrent liabilities and the $17,000 of equity.

That part of the current assets not financed by the current liabilities is called **working capital**. Working capital is therefore the difference between current assets and current liabilities. In the example given above, working capital is:

$$\$10,000 - \$4,000 = \$6,000.$$

SOURCES OF CAPITAL

To highlight how working capital and the noncurrent assets were financed, we can rearrange the items on the balance sheet as follows:

LOUGEE COMPANY

Sources and Uses of Permanent Capital
as of December 31, 19x1

Uses of Capital		Sources of Capital	
Working capital..........................	$ 6,000	Noncurrent liabilities................	$ 9,000
Noncurrent assets......................	20,000	Equity...	17,000
Total uses	$26,000	Total sources	$26,000

The right-hand side of the balance sheet given above shows the sources of capital used to finance the working capital and the noncurrent assets. Collectively, these sources are called **permanent capital**. As the balance sheet indicates, there are two sources of permanent capital: (1) Noncurrent liabilities and (2) Equity. The total of these two sources is $26,000, and they are used to finance assets that also total $26,000.

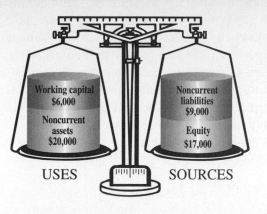

Working capital $6,000	Noncurrent liabilities $9,000
Noncurrent assets $20,000	Equity $17,000
USES	SOURCES

In this part we describe the two types of permanent capital and how they are recorded in the accounts. Although these items are called "capital," they are more accurately labelled "sources of capital."

DEBT CAPITAL

Although most liabilities are debts, the term **debt capital** refers only to noncurrent liabilities. Debt capital therefore refers to liabilities that come due sometime after one year.

A common source of debt capital is the issuance of **bonds**. A bond is a written promise to pay someone who lends money to the entity. Since a bond usually is a noncurrent liability, the payments are due sometime after one year. The total amount of loan that must be repaid is specified on the face of a bond and is termed the **face amount**. If Green Company issues ten-year bonds whose face amounts total $100,000, Green Company has a liability, Bonds Payable, of $100,000.

(If the entity does not receive cash equal to the face amount of the bonds, there are accounting complications not discussed in this introductory book.)

Example. Suppose that Green Company receives $100,000 cash from the issuance of bonds that have a face amount of $100,000. The journal entry necessary to record the effect of this transaction on the Cash and Bonds Payable accounts follows:

```
Dr. Cash . . . . . . . . . . . . . . . . . 100,000
    Cr. Bonds Payable . . . . . .            100,000
```

When they are issued, the bonds are noncurrent liabilities. However, as time passes and the due date becomes less than one year, a bond becomes a current liability. In 19x1, a bond that is due on January 1, 19x3, would be a noncurrent liability. In 19x2 the same bond would be a current liability.

When an entity issues bonds, it assumes two obligations. It is obligated (1) to repay the face amount, the **principal**, on the due date; and (2) to pay **interest**, usually at semiannual intervals (i.e., twice a year). The obligation to pay the principal is usually a noncurrent liability. The liability for interest that has been earned by the bondholders but is unpaid is a current liability.

Interest on bonds is an expense and is recognized as such in the accounting period to which the interest applies.

> **Example.** If in January 19x2 an entity makes a semiannual interest payment of $3,000 to cover the last six months of 19x1, this interest expense should be recognized in 19x1. This is required by the matching concept.
>
> The $3,000 of unpaid interest that was an expense in 19x1 is recorded in 19x1 by the following entry.

```
Dr. Interest Expense ......    3,000
    Cr. Interest Payable ...            3,000
```

> In 19x2, when this interest was paid to the bondholders, the following entry would be made.

```
Dr. Interest Payable ......    3,000
    Cr. Cash ..............            3,000
```

As the above entries indicate, the liability for the principal payment is the total face value of the bond, but the interest liability is the amount of interest expense incurred but unpaid.

Some bonds, called **zero-coupon bonds**, do not pay interest. The buyer purchases them for less than the principal amount, and the entity promises to pay the principal amount on the due date. The buyer's return (i.e., income) is therefore the difference between the purchase price and the principal amount.

EQUITY: PAID-IN CAPITAL

The other source of permanent capital is **equity capital**.

Unlike a bond, which is a promise to pay and therefore is a liability, equity is an ownership interest in the entity, and the entity does not promise to pay equity investors anything. Equity is not a liability.

As noted in earlier parts, there are two sources of equity capital:

1. Amounts paid in by equity investors, who are the entity's owners, which are called Paid-in Capital.

2. Amounts generated by the profitable operation of the entity, which are called Retained Earnings.

TYPES OF EQUITY CAPITAL

Some entities do not report these two sources separately. An unincorporated business owned by a single person is called a **proprietorship**. The equity item in a proprietorship is often reported by giving the proprietor's name, followed by the word Capital.

> *Example.* Mary Green is the proprietor of Green's Market. Green's Market has equity of $10,000. The owner's equity item would appear as:
>
> Mary Green, Capital............... $10,000

A **partnership** is an unincorporated business owned by two or more persons jointly. If there are only a few partners, the equity of each might be shown separately.

> *Example.* John Black and Henry Brown are equal partners in a laundry business. On December 31, 19x1, the equity in the business totalled $100,000. The equity might be reported on that date as follows:
>
> John Black, Capital................ $ 50,000
>
> Henry Brown, Capital............ 50,000
>
> Total equity $100,000

Equity in a partnership consists of capital paid-in by owners, plus earnings retained in the business. Thus the item "John Black, Capital, $50,000" means John Black's ownership interest in the assets is $50,000, including the capital he paid in plus his share of retained earnings.

Owners of a **corporation** are called **shareholders** because they hold shares of the corporation's stock. The equity section of a corporation's balance sheet is therefore labeled shareholder equity.

There are two types of shareholders: **common shareholders** and **preferred shareholders**. The stock held by the former is called common stock, and that held by the latter is called preferred stock. We shall first describe accounting for common stock.

COMMON STOCK

Some stock is issued with a specific amount printed on the face of each certificate. This amount is called the **par value**. In the stock certificate shown below, for example, the par value is $1, as indicated in the upper right corner.

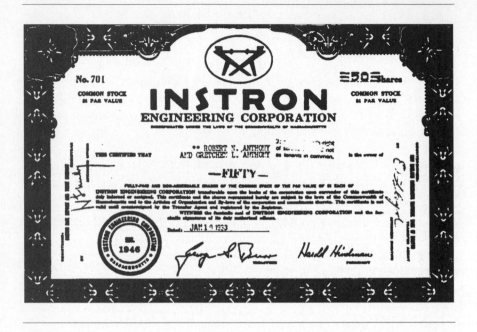

Strangely, the par value of stock has practically no significance. It is a holdover from the days when shareholders were liable if they purchased stock for less than its par value. In order to avoid this liability, stock today is always issued for much more than its par value. Nevertheless, the par value of stock continues to be reported on the balance sheet.

The amount that the shareholders paid the corporation in exchange for their stock is **paid-in capital**. The difference between par value and the total paid-in capital is called **additional paid-in capital**.

Example. Jones paid $10,000 cash to Marple Company and received 1,000 shares of its $1 par-value common stock. Marple Company would make the following journal entry for this transaction.

```
Dr. Cash .................  10,000
    Cr. Common stock .......         1,000
    Cr. Additional paid-in capital   9,000
```

If Jones's payment of $10,000 were the only equity transaction, this section of the Marple Company balance sheet would appear as follows:

Common stock	$ 1,000
Additional paid-in capital	9,000
Total paid-in capital	$10,000

Not all stocks have a par value. For these **no-par-value stocks**, the directors state a value. This value, called the **stated value**, is usually set close to the amount that the corporation actually receives from the issuance of the stock. The difference between the stated value and the cash received is Additional Paid-in Capital, just as in the case of par-value stock.

When a corporation is formed, its directors vote to **authorize** a certain number of shares of stock and to **issue** some of this authorized stock to investors. Thus, at any given time the amount of stock authorized is usually larger than the amount issued.

A corporation may buy back some of the stock that it had previously issued. Such stock is called **treasury stock**. The **outstanding stock** consists of the issued stock less the treasury stock. If a company issues 100,000 shares and buys back 15,000 shares, its treasury stock is 15,000 shares, and its outstanding stock is 85,000 shares.

The balance sheet amount for common stock is the amount for the number of shares of stock outstanding.

Example. Maxim Company has authorized 100,000 shares of stock. It has issued 60,000 shares, for which it received the stated value of $10 per share. As of December 31, 19x1, it has bought back 10,000 shares, paying $10 per share. These shares are its treasury stock. The balance sheet amount for common stock is $500,000 [(60,000 ∗ $10) − (10,000 ∗ $10)].

Shareholders may sell their stock to other investors. Such sales do not affect the balance sheet of the corporation. This is an example of the entity concept.

When shareholders sell their stock to other investors, the price at which the sale takes place is determined in the **marketplace**. The market value of a company's stock has no necessary relation to its par value, its stated value, or the amount of paid-in capital.

The amount reported as total equity is equal to total assets less total liabilities. On the balance sheet, this is not likely to equal the total market value of all stock outstanding. Accounting does not report the market value of the shareholders' equity.

PREFERRED STOCK

Some corporations issue stock that gives its owners preferential treatment over the common shareholders. Such stock is called **preferred stock**.

Usually preferred shareholders have a preferential claim over the common shareholders for the par value of their stock. Thus, if the corporation were liquidated, the owner of 500 shares of $100 preferred stock would get $50,000 before the common shareholders got anything.

Although par value of common stock has practically no significance, preferred stock usually does have a preferential claim on assets equal to its par value, and its par value therefore has some significance.

Preferred shareholders usually have preference for a stated amount of annual dividends. If Pemi Corporation issued $100,000 of 9% preferred stock, no dividend can be paid to common shareholders until the preferred shareholders have received their dividend of 9% of $100,000, amounting to $9,000 a year.

RETAINED EARNINGS AND DIVIDENDS

The net income of a period increases equity. The directors may vote to distribute money to the shareholders in the form of **dividends**. Dividends decrease equity.

The Retained Earnings account increases by the amount of net income each period and decreases by the amount of dividends. Thus, if Retained Earnings are $100,000 at the start of a period during which a dividend of $20,000 is declared and during which net income is $30,000, Retained Earnings will be $110,000 at the close of the period.

Net income refers to the increase in equity in one year, whereas **retained earnings** refers to the net increases (after deduction of dividends) over the life of the corporation to date.

Equity is sometimes called "net worth." This term suggests that the amount shows what the owners' claim on the assets is *worth*. Because the amounts reported on the assets side of the balance sheet do not represent the real worth of these assets, this suggestion is wrong. The **worth** of a company's stock is what people will pay for it. This is the market price of the stock, which does not appear anywhere on the balance sheet.

TYPES OF STOCK TRANSACTIONS
Cash Dividend

Suppose that a dividend of $5,000 is declared and paid in cash. The journal entry necessary to record the effect of this transaction on the Cash and Retained Earnings accounts follows:

```
Dr. Retained Earnings........    5,000
    Cr. Cash.................            5,000
```

A cash dividend decreases the total amount of equity, but leaves the total number of shares outstanding unchanged.

Stock Dividend

Dividends are usually paid in the form of cash. Sometimes, however, the dividend consists of shares of stock in the corporation. The latter is called a **stock dividend**.

In a typical stock dividend, shareholders are issued additional shares of common stock amounting to 5% or 10% of the total they currently own. In a 10% stock dividend, for example, the holder of 900 shares receives 90 additional shares of stock.

Since the number of shares received by each shareholder in a stock dividend is proportional to the number of shares that each shareholder currently owns, the percentage of the total equity owned by each stockholder stays the same as a result of a stock dividend.

When a dividend of common stock is declared, Retained Earnings is decreased and Additional Paid-in Capital is increased by the amount of the dividend. A dividend of $10,000 of common stock is recorded as:

```
Dr. Retained Earnings........    10,000
    Cr. Additional Paid-in Capital       10,000
```

In a stock dividend, the Retained Earnings account decreases by an amount equal to the increase in the Additional Paid-in Capital account; therefore the total amount of equity does not change, even though the total number of shares outstanding increases.

Stock Split

A corporation may decide to exchange the number of shares outstanding for other shares, often two or more times the existing number. The process is called a **stock split**. In a three-for-one stock split, for example, each shareholder receives three new shares for each old share held. The total number of shares outstanding therefore increases.

A stock split does not affect the total amount of equity or the percentage of stock held by each shareholder. A shareholder who owns 1% of the stock before a stock split owns 1% of it afterwards, and owns more shares.

In summary:

	Total amount of equity	Total number of shares outstanding
Cash dividend	decreases	unchanged
Stock dividend	unchanged	increases
Stock split	unchanged	increases

The equity section of a corporation's balance sheet has these main items:

1. Paid-in Capital from stock that has preference, called preferred stock.

2. Paid-in Capital from common stock, which consists of (a) the par or stated value of the number of shares outstanding, plus (b) the additional amount paid for the stock, called Additional Paid-in Capital.

3. Retained Earnings, which is the difference between net income and dividends since the corporation began.

BALANCE BETWEEN DEBT AND EQUITY CAPITAL

A corporation obtains some capital from retained earnings. In addition, it obtains capital from the issuance of stock, which is equity capital, and from the issuance of bonds, which is debt capital.

A corporation has no fixed obligations to its common shareholders; that is, the company need not declare dividends each year, and need not repay the amount the shareholders have invested.

A company has two fixed obligations to its bondholders, however:

- Payment of interest.

- Repayment of principal.

If the company fails to pay either the interest or the principal when due, the bondholders may force the company into bankruptcy. Bonds are a more risky method of raising capital by the corporation than stock; that is, debt capital is a more risky source of capital than equity capital.

Bonds are an obligation of the company that issues them, but stocks are not an obligation. Therefore, *investors* have more risk if they invest in a company's stock than if they invest in the bonds of the same company. They are not sure of getting either dividends or repayment of their investment. Investors therefore expect a higher return from an investment in stock than from an investment in bonds in the same company.

For example, if a company's bonds had an interest rate of 9%, investors would invest in its stock only if they expected that the return on stock would be considerably more than 9%. (The expected return on stock consists of both expected dividends and an expected increase in the market value of the stock.)

Thus, from the viewpoint of the issuing company, stock, which is equity capital, is a more expensive source of capital than bonds, which are debt capital.

The principal differences between debt capital and equity capital can be summarized as:

	Bonds (Debt)	Stock (Equity)
Annual payments required	Yes	No
Principal payments required	Yes	No
Risk to the entity is	High	Low
But its cost is relatively	Low	High

In deciding on its permanent capital structure, a company must decide on the proper balance between debt capital, which has a relatively high risk and a relatively low cost, and equity capital, which has a relatively low risk and a relatively high cost.

A company runs the risk of going bankrupt if it has too high a proportion of debt capital. A company pays an unnecessarily high cost for its permanent capital if it has too high a proportion of equity capital.

A company that obtains a high proportion of its permanent capital from debt is said to be **highly leveraged**. If such a company does not get into financial difficulty, it will earn a high return for its equity investors, because each dollar of debt capital takes the place of a more expensive dollar of equity capital.

However, highly leveraged companies are risky because the high proportion of debt capital and the associated requirement to pay interest increases the chance that the company will not be able to meet its obligations.

In this introductory treatment, we focus on the basic differences between common stock and bonds. Some additional points worth noting:

1. The interest on bonds is a tax-deductible expense to the corporation. If the annual interest expense on a 9% bond is $90,000, the corporation's taxable income is reduced by $90,000. At a tax rate of 40%,

the net cost to the corporation is then only 60% of $90,000, or $54,000; the effective interest cost is 5.4% (i.e., 60% of 9%).

2. Preferred stock has risk and cost characteristics that are in between common stocks and bonds. However, dividends on preferred stock do not reduce a corporation's taxable income. Preferred stock is not a widely used source of capital.

3. In recent years, there has been a tremendous increase in the types of debt and equity securities. New financial instruments are structured with risk and cost characteristics designed to meet the needs of various types of investors.

Debt ratio. A common way of measuring the relative amount of debt and equity capital is the **debt ratio**, which is the ratio of debt capital to total permanent capital. Recall that **debt capital** is another name for noncurrent liabilities. Equity capital consists of Paid-in Capital plus Retained Earnings.

Earlier we worked with the following permanent capital structure:

LOUGEE COMPANY

Sources and Uses of Permanent Capital
as of December 31, 19x1

Uses of Capital		Sources of Capital	
Working capital..........................	$ 6,000	Noncurrent liabilities................	$ 9,000
Noncurrent assets......................	20,000	Equity...	17,000
Total uses	$26,000	Total sources	$26,000

The debt ratio for Lougee Company can be calculated as

$$\frac{\text{Debt capital (noncurrent liabilities)}}{\text{Debt capital + equity capital}} = \frac{\$9,000}{\$26,000} = 35\%$$

Most industrial companies have a debt ratio of less than 50%. Lougee Company is in this category.

CONSOLIDATED FINANCIAL STATEMENTS

If one corporation owns more than 50% of the stock in another corporation, it can control the affairs of that corporation because it can outvote all other owners. Many businesses consist of a number of corporations that are legally separate entities but, because they are controlled by one corporation, are part of a single "family." A corporation which controls one or more other corporations is called the **parent**, and the controlled corporations are called **subsidiaries**.

Example. Palm Company owns 100% of the stock of Sea Company, 60% of the stock of Sand Company, and 40% of the stock of Gray Company. The **parent** company is Palm Company. The **subsidiaries** are Sea Company and Sand Company.

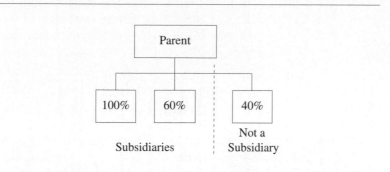

Since the management of the parent, Palm Company, controls the activities of Sea Company and Sand Company, these three companies operate as a single entity. The entity concept requires that a set of financial statements be prepared for this family.

Each corporation is a legal entity with its own financial statements. The set of financial statements for the whole family brings together, or *consolidates*, these separate statements. The set for the whole family is therefore called **consolidated financial statements**.

For example, if Palm Company has $10,000 cash, Sea Company has $5,000 cash, and Sand Company has $4,000 cash, the whole family has $19,000 cash, and this amount would be reported on the consolidated balance sheet.

An entity earns income by making sales to outside customers. It cannot earn income by dealing with itself. Corporations in the consolidated family may buy from and sell to one another. Transactions between members of the family do not earn income for the consolidated entity. The effect of these **intrafamily transactions** therefore must be eliminated from the consolidated statements.

Example. In 19x1, Palm Company had sales revenue of $1,000,000. Sea Company had sales revenue of $200,000, and Sand Company had sales revenue of $400,000. Palm Company sold $30,000 of products to Sea Company. All other sales were to outside customers. On the consolidated income statement, the amount of sales reported would be $1,570,000 (= 1,000,000 + 200,000 + 400,000 − 30,000 of intrafamily sales).

Intrafamily transactions are also eliminated from the consolidated balance sheet. For example, if Sand Company owed Palm Company $10,000, this amount would appear as Accounts Receivable on the balance sheet of Palm Company and as Accounts Payable on the balance sheet of Sand Company. On the consolidated balance sheet, the Accounts Receivable and Accounts Payable would each be $10,000 less than the sum of these amounts on the balance sheets of each of the family members.

The balance sheet of Palm Company reports as an asset the Sand Company and Sea Company stock that it owns. This asset must be eliminated from the consolidated balance sheet. On the balance sheets of the subsidiaries, the corresponding amounts are reported as equity, and these amounts are also eliminated.

> **Example.** Palm Company owns 60% of the stock of Sand Company. This stock was reported on the balance sheet of Palm Company as an asset, Investment in Subsidiaries, at $60,000. The equity of Sand Corporation is $100,000. On the consolidated balance sheet, the $60,000 asset would be eliminated, and because debits must equal credits, $60,000 of Sand Company's equity also would be eliminated.

Palm Company owns 40% of Gray Company stock. This asset is listed on Palm Company's balance sheet at $100,000. It would not be eliminated from the consolidated balance sheet, because only companies of which the parent owns more than 50% are consolidated.

Palm Company owns 60% of Sand Company's stock, which is a majority of the stock. Other shareholders own the other 40% of Sand Company stock; they are minority shareholders. They have an interest in the consolidated entity, and this interest is reported on the liabilities and equity side of the consolidated balance sheet. It is labeled **minority interest**.

The consolidated financial statements report on the entity called "Palm Company and Subsidiaries." This family of corporations is an economic entity, but it is not a legal entity.

Many corporations have subsidiaries. Since the consolidated financial statements give the best information about the economic entity, many published financial statements are consolidated financial statements. In an entity with dozens of subsidiaries, some of which have their own subsidiaries, eliminating the intrafamily transactions is a complicated task. Only the general principles have been described here.

KEY POINTS TO REMEMBER

- A company obtains its permanent capital from two sources: (1) debt (i.e., noncurrent liabilities) and (2) equity. It uses this capital to finance (1) working capital (i.e., current assets – current liabilities) and (2) noncurrent assets.

- Most debt capital is obtained by issuing bonds. Bonds obligate the company to pay interest and to repay the principal when it is due.

- Equity capital is obtained by (1) issuing shares of stock and (2) retaining earnings.

- The amount of capital obtained from preferred and common shareholders is the amount they paid in. The par, or stated, value of common stock is not an important number today, but it is still reported on the balance sheet.

- Cash dividends decrease the amount of equity capital. Stock dividends or stock splits do not affect the total equity.

- Retained earnings are total earnings (i.e., net income) since the entity began operations, less total dividends. (A net loss, of course, results in a decrease in retained earnings.)

- Although sometimes called "net worth," the amount of owners' equity does *not* show what the owners' interest is worth.

- In deciding on its permanent capital structure, a company attempts to strike the right balance between (1) risky but low-cost debt capital and (2) less risky but high-cost equity capital. The balance in a given company is indicated by its debt ratio.

- Many companies have subsidiaries. The economic entity is a family consisting of the parent and the subsidiaries in which it owns more than 50% of the stock. Consolidated financial statements are prepared for such an economic entity by combining their separate financial statements and eliminating transactions among members of the family.

- The consolidated balance sheet reports all the assets owned by the consolidated entity and all the claims of parties outside the family.

- The consolidated income statement reports only revenues from sales to outside parties and expenses resulting from costs incurred with outside parties. Intrafamily revenues and expenses are eliminated.

PART 10

The Statement of Cash Flows

This part describes:
* What a statement of cash flows is.
* How it differs from an income statement.
* The meaning of the operating items.
* The content of the investing and financing sections.
* The relationship of depreciation to cash flow.
* Uses of the statement of cash flows.

A company must prepare three financial statements. We described two of them in earlier parts. The balance sheet reports the financial status of the company as of the end of each accounting period. The income statement reports financial performance during the period. In this part, we describe the third required statement. It reports the flow of cash during the accounting period, and it is therefore called the **statement of cash flows**.

Both the income statement and the cash flow statement report flows during the period. The difference is that the income statement reports flows on the **accrual** basis; that is, inflows are measured as revenues and outflows are measured as expenses. By contrast, the cash flow statement reports inflows and outflows of cash. The income statement focuses on profitability, while the cash flow statement focuses on liquidity.

Example. Assume that an entity sold goods for $1,000 on May 1, and the customer paid $1,000 for these goods on June 1. The entity's cash inflow on May 1 would be $0, while its revenue in May would be $1,000. Its cash inflow on June 1 would be $1,000, while its revenue in June would be $0. In June, the balance sheet would show the cash received, while Accounts Receivable would be reduced as the customer pays the $1,000. As we discussed earlier, an entity's revenues and expenses do not necessarily match its cash receipts and disbursements in that period.

There are two acceptable methods of preparing the cash flow statement. One is to summarize the debits and credits (inflows and outflows) to the Cash account directly; it is therefore called the **direct method**. Most companies use the other method, which is called the **indirect method**.

The indirect method is more widely used because it shows the relationship between the income statement and the balance sheet and therefore aids in the analysis of these statements. The indirect method analyzes income statement and balance sheet items to determine whether the offsetting entries to the debits and credits to these accounts involved credits or debits to Cash. If there was a credit to Cash, there was an outflow of cash. If there was a debit to Cash, there was an inflow of cash.

In this part, we develop a cash flow statement for Arlen Company, using the indirect method and the balance sheet and income statement information in Exhibit 10.1. This statement is given in Exhibit 10.2.

In the cash flow statement, "cash" includes not only money, but also assets that are almost the same as money, such as certificates of deposit and money market accounts. These are equivalent to cash and are called **cash equivalents**.

The cash flow statement in Exhibit 10.2 consists of three sections. We will describe the first section, called "Cash Flow from Operating Activities," in some detail. We will describe the other two sections, called "Cash Flow from Investing Activities" and "Cash Flow from Financing Activities," together because the same principles apply to both. The principal purpose of this part is to show the relationship between the accrual accounting numbers and cash. The individual items on the cash flow statement are largely self explanatory.

CASH FLOW FROM OPERATING ACTIVITIES

The first section of the cash flow statement reports how much cash was generated by the operating activities of the period; that is, the day-to-day activities that bring cash in from customers and pay cash out to employees and suppliers. To do this, we must first convert net income—the bottom line of the income statement—from an accrual basis to a cash basis.

EXHIBIT 10.1

ARLEN COMPANY
Balance Sheets (000 Omitted)

Assets

	As of December 31	
	19x2	19x1
Current assets		
Cash	$ 20	$ 7
Accounts receivable	40	42
Inventory	60	56
Prepaid expenses	20	20
Total current assets	140	125
Noncurrent assets		
Land	$ 30	$ 30
Plant, at cost $120	$108	
Less accumulated depreciation..... 70	50	64	44
Goodwill and patents	10	10
Total assets	230	209

Liabilities and Equity

Current liabilities		
Accounts payable	$ 30	$ 33
Accrued wages	10	6
Income taxes payable	20	20
Total current liabilities	60	59
Noncurrent liabilities		
Mortgage bonds payable	40	34
Total liabilities	100	93
Shareholder equity		
Paid-in capital (4,800 shares outstanding)	$ 60	$ 60
Retained earnings	70	56
Total shareholder equity	130	116
Total liabilities and equity	230	209

Income Statement, 19x2 (000 Omitted)

		Percentage
Sales revenue	$300	100.0
Less cost of sales	− 180	60.0
Gross margin	120	40.0
Less depreciation expense	− 6	2.0
Other expenses	− 72	24.0
Earnings before interest and taxes	42	14.0
Interest expense	− 5	1.7
Earnings before income taxes	37	12.3
Provision for income taxes	− 13	4.3
Net income	24	8.0
Less dividends	− 10	
Addition to equity	14	

EXHIBIT 10.2

ARLEN COMPANY

Statement of Cash Flows, 19x2

Cash Flow from Operating Activities

Net income		$24
Decrease in accounts receivable	$ 2	
Increase in inventory	(4)	
Decrease in accounts payable	(3)	
Increase in accrued wages	4	
Effect of change in working capital	(1)	
Depreciation expense	6	
Total adjustments to net income		5
Total cash flow from operations		29

Cash Flow from Investing Activities

Purchase of Plant		(12)

Cash Flow from Financing Activities

Issuance of long-term debt	6	
Dividends paid	(10)	(4)
Net increase in cash and cash equivalents		$13

Note: Parentheses indicate decreases in cash.

Net income is the difference between revenues and expenses. "Cash Flow from Operating Activities" is the difference between operating cash inflows and operating cash outflows. To find the amount of cash flow from operating activities, we make two types of adjustments to net income: (1) for depreciation and other expenses that *never* require an outflow of cash and (2) for changes in working capital accounts.

Depreciation Expense

According to its balance sheet (Exhibit 10.1), Arlen Company owned Plant, most of which it had acquired prior to 19x2, at a cost of $108,000. The cash outflow for these assets occurred prior to 19x2.

According to its income statement, Arlen Company had depreciation expense of $6,000 in 19x2. Depreciation writes off a portion of the cost of fixed assets. The cash outflow for the assets on hand at the beginning of 19x2 occurred in earlier years; this depreciation expense therefore was *not* a cash outflow in 19x2.

Although depreciation expense is subtracted from revenue in arriving at net income, it is not a cash outflow. Net income is $6,000 less than it would have been with no depreciation expense. Therefore, in Exhibit 10.2 net income is adjusted to a cash basis by adding $6,000 to net income.

Suppose that Arlen Company had decided to charge depreciation expense of $10,000, rather than $6,000, in 19x2, but made no other changes in the accounts. The cash flow from operating activities would then be the same as the amount reported in Exhibit 10.2. This occurs because, if depreciation expense was $4,000 higher than the amount reported in Exhibit 10.1, net income would be $4,000 lower than the amount reported. The $4,000 increase in depreciation expense would offset exactly the $4,000 decrease in net income. Cash flow would therefore be the same as the amount reported in Exhibit 10.2.

(Recall that the Cash account is not changed by the journal entry that records depreciation expense:

```
Dr. Depreciation Expense
    Cr. Accumulated Depreciation)
```

Amortization of intangible assets, write-off of losses, and other non-cash expenses also are added to net income to convert net income to cash flow from operating activities.

Adjustments for Changes in Working Capital

Cash, inventory, accounts receivable, and similar items that will be converted into cash in the near future are current assets. Wages payable, accounts payable, and similar obligations that are due in the near future are current liabilities. The difference between current assets and current liabilities is **working capital**. Operating activities—such as making sales, purchasing materials for inventory, and incurring production, selling, and administrative expenses—are the principal causes of changes in working capital items. We will analyze the asset items first, and follow with an analysis of liability items.

Although cash is, of course, an item of working capital, we exclude it here because we want to analyze the effect of changes in the other working capital accounts on cash.

Changes in Current Assets

No Change in Balance. If all revenues in 19x2 were from cash sales, cash inflows would be the same amount as revenues; that is, if sales revenues were $300,000, cash inflows would be $300,000. However, in most companies, some sales are made to credit customers. These sales are first reported as the current asset, Accounts Receivable. The company will receive cash later on, when customers pay their bills.

In Arlen Company, all sales were credit sales. If sales in 19x2 were $300,000, Revenues would be $300,000, and Accounts Receivable would increase by $300,000 when these sales were made.

The journal entry summarizing the above transaction would be (omitting 000):

```
Dr. Accounts Receivable......      300
    Cr. Revenues .............            300
```

If, in 19x2, Arlen Company received $300,000 cash from credit customers, Cash would increase and Accounts Receivable would decrease, as summarized in the following journal entry:

```
Dr. Cash....................      300
    Cr. Accounts Receivable...            300
```

The above two journal entries are posted to the following ledger accounts:

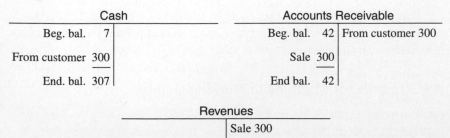

Cash		Accounts Receivable	
Beg. bal. 7		Beg. bal. 42	From customer 300
From customer 300		Sale 300	
End. bal. 307		End bal. 42	

Revenues	
	Sale 300

As the above accounts show, when the balance in Accounts Receivable does not change, the increase in cash is the same as the sales revenues.

This is the case with all working capital accounts. If the beginning balance is the same as the ending balance, an adjustment from the accrual basis to the cash basis is not necessary.

Current Asset Balance Decreased. Now, consider what the account balances would have been if Arlen Company had revenues of $300,000, but had received $302,000 cash from customers. These transactions are entered in the following accounts:

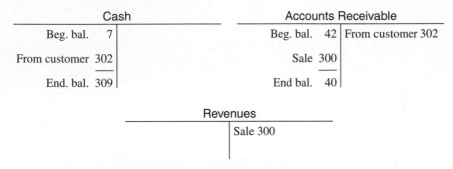

Cash			Accounts Receivable		
Beg. bal.	7		Beg. bal.	42	From customer 302
From customer	302		Sale	300	
End. bal.	309		End bal.	40	

Revenues	
	Sale 300

The above accounts show that in this situation, the ending balance of Cash would have been $2,000 larger than what the Cash balance was when cash receipts equaled sales revenues, as shown earlier. The Accounts Receivable balance would have been $2,000 smaller than the balance when cash receipts equaled sales revenues. Revenues in 19x2 would still have been $300,000.

This example shows that if the ending balance in Accounts Receivable was *less* than its beginning balance, the increase in Cash would be *more* than the amount of Revenues. Part of the increase in Cash would be the result of decreasing Accounts Receivable. Put another way, Cash increased partly because more old customers paid their bills and partly because of sales to new customers. This is what happened in Arlen Company.

Because the increase in Cash was more than the amount of Revenues, we must add to net income the amount by which Cash was greater than Revenues. This is $2,000, which is the amount entered in Exhibit 10.2.

Current Asset Balance Increased. If Accounts Receivable had increased during the period, the adjustment of net income would be the opposite; that is, an increase in a non-cash current asset leads to an adjustment that subtracts from net income in order to find the cash flow from operations.

As shown in Exhibit 10.1, the beginning balance in Inventory was $56,000, and the ending balance was $60,000, which shows that this asset increased by $4,000 during the year. This change had the opposite effect on Cash from the effect of the change in Accounts Receivable. Therefore, we must subtract from net income to arrive at the change in cash. The $4,000 subtraction is shown in Exhibit 10.2.

Analysis with Diagrams. Let's repeat this analysis, this time using diagrams. The situations illustrated are those in which the beginning balance of Accounts Receivable was $100,000 and additions during the year from sales to customers (revenues) were $800,000. The following diagram shows the situation in which the ending balance in Accounts Receivable was the same as the balance at the beginning of the year.

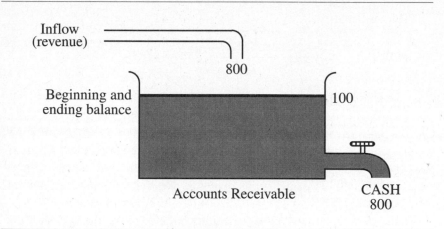

We calculate the inflow to Cash as:

Beginning balance	$ 100
Ending balance	– 100
Change	0
Revenue	800
Inflow to Cash	800

Thus, if the balance in Accounts Receivable is unchanged, the inflow to Cash is the same amount as revenue and an adjustment is not necessary.

Next, consider the situation in which the ending balance in Accounts Receivable was less than the beginning balance, as illustrated in the following diagram:

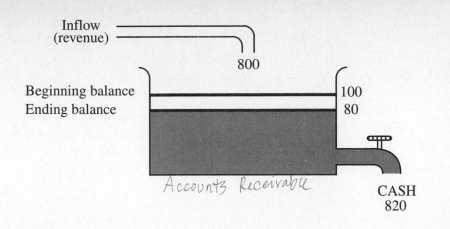

We calculate the inflow to Cash as:

Beginning balance	$ 100
Ending balance	− 80
Change	20
Revenue	800
Inflow to Cash	820

Thus, if the ending balance in Accounts Receivable is less than the beginning balance, the inflow to Cash is more than the amount of revenue, and so we must add to net income in order to show the effect on cash.

Finally, consider the situation in which the ending balance in Accounts Receivable was greater than the beginning balance, as illustrated in the following diagram:

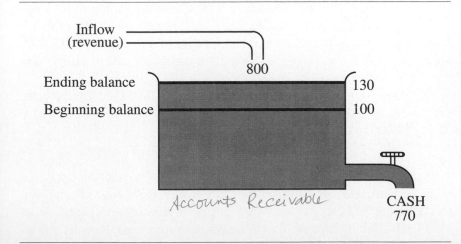

Beginning balance	$ 100
Ending balance	– 130
Change	(30)
Revenue	800
Inflow to Cash	770

Thus, if the ending balance in Accounts Receivable is greater than the beginning balance, the inflow to Cash is less than the amount of revenue, and we subtract from net income in order to show the effect on cash.

An easy way to remember whether the impact on Cash (and hence the adjustment to net income) is an addition or a subtraction is to pretend that only that account and Cash exist. For example, if Cash and Accounts Receivable were the only accounts, a decrease in Accounts Receivable would have to mean an increase in Cash. This follows from the fundamental accounting equation: Assets = Liabilities + Equity. To keep this equation in balance, a decrease in Accounts Receivable would necessarily mean an equal increase in Cash, again assuming that these were the only two accounts involved.

A change in a current asset may not have an immediate effect on Cash. For example, an increase in Inventory may be accompanied by an increase in Accounts Payable. However, the ultimate effect on Cash is as described, and the effect on other accounts will be considered when we analyze those accounts.

Changes in Current Liabilities

Changes in current liabilities have the opposite effect on Cash from changes in current assets. An increase in a current liability requires that the net income amount be adjusted to a cash basis by adding to it. A decrease in a current liability requires that the adjustment be a subtraction.

Exhibit 10.1 shows that Accounts Payable decreased by $3,000. Therefore, in Exhibit 10.2 net income is adjusted to a cash basis by subtracting $3,000.

Exhibit 10.1 shows that Accrued Wages increased by $4,000. Therefore, in Exhibit 10.2 net income is adjusted to a cash basis by adding $4,000 to it.

Net Effect of Working Capital Changes

Using Exhibit 10.2, we can find the net effect of these four adjustments on converting net income to a cash basis: there was a net decrease of $1,000. Exhibit 10.2 shows that although cash increased, the increase in Cash was $1,000 less than net income.

In summary, an increase in current assets means that more of the cash inflow was tied up in accounts receivable, inventory, and/or other current assets, with a corresponding decrease in cash. This is why, in times when cash is low, a business tries to keep the other current assets as low as feasible.

Also, an increase in current liabilities means that more cash was freed up. The cash not paid to suppliers is still in the Cash account. This is why, in times when cash is low, a business tries to keep current liabilities as high as feasible.

Users of financial statements need to understand these relationships, but there is no need to memorize them. The cash flow statement gives the net effect of each of the four types of adjustments in working capital items. The following summarizes them:

Change	Adjustment to Net Income
Decrease in a current asset	add
Increase in a current asset	subtract
Decrease in a current liability	subtract
Increase in a current liability	add

Remember: These adjustments are made to convert the net income number to a cash basis. The net income number, as reported on the income statement, is not changed.

To complete the "Cash Flows from Operating Activities" section of Exhibit 10.2, we see that cash flow from operating activities was $29,000.

Note that the $6,000 adjustment for depreciation expense is larger than the net amount of all the working capital adjustments. This is the case in many companies, especially manufacturing companies that have relatively large amounts of fixed assets.

As a shortcut, therefore, some analysts arrive at the operating cash flow simply by adding depreciation expense to net income. They disregard changes in working capital on the assumption that these changes net out to a minor amount. This shortcut may give the impression that depreciation is a cash flow. Such an impression is erroneous.

Summary of Operating Adjustments

If the total amount of working capital (excluding cash) did not change, and if there were no non-cash expenses, such as depreciation, cash flow from operations would be the same as net income.

If working capital decreased, cash flow from operations will be higher than net income. Cash was released from working capital accounts.

If working capital increased, cash flow from operations will be lower than net income. More cash was tied up in working capital accounts.

If there was depreciation expense, cash flow from operations will be higher than net income.

INVESTING AND FINANCING FLOWS

Exhibit 10.2 shows that in addition to cash flows from operating activities, there are two other categories on a cash flow statement: cash flows from investing activities and cash flows from financing activities.

Investing Activities

When a company invests in additional property or plant, the amount involved is a cash outflow from the company. The amount may not be an immediate net decrease in cash because the payment of cash may have been offset by borrowing an equal amount. Nevertheless, it is recorded as a cash outflow, and the amount of the borrowing is recorded separately as a financing activity.

As shown in Exhibit 10.1, Arlen Company had Plant at the beginning of 19x2 that had cost $108,000. It had $120,000 of Plant at the end of 19x2. As shown in Exhibit 10.2, the increase of $12,000 was an investing activity in 19x2. (The parentheses indicate that this was a cash outflow.)

The amount of *new* plant acquired may have been more than $12,000, say $15,000; the difference of $3,000 would represent cash obtained from the sale of existing plant. Both transactions are investing activities. However, we cannot obtain a breakdown of the amount from the available information.

Similarly, if the Plant account decreased, representing the sale of plant assets, there would have been an inflow of cash.

Financing Activities

Companies may obtain cash by issuing debt securities, such as bonds. Issuing debt securities is a financing activity.

As shown in Exhibit 10.2, Arlen Company had a liability, mortgage bonds. The amount was $34,000 at the beginning of 19x2 and $40,000 at the end of 19x2. The increase of $6,000 showed that Arlen Company issued bonds of this amount. This was a financing activity. It represented an increase in cash as shown in Exhibit 10.2.

Similar to the plant transaction discussed earlier, the amount of new bonds issued may have been more than $6,000. Part of the new issue may have been used to pay off existing bonds. The issuance of, and redemption of, bonds are financing activities.

The borrowings reported in the financing section are long-term borrowings. Short-term borrowings are current liabilities; changes in them are reported in the section on Cash Flow from Operating Activities. (There is one exception. The current portion of long-term debt is a current liability. However, for the purpose of cash flow analysis, it is reported as a financing activity.)

Issuance of additional shares of a company's stock is also a financing activity. Exhibit 10.1 shows that Arlen Company's Paid-in Capital was $60,000 at the beginning of 19x2 and $60,000 at the end of 19x2. Evidently, the company did not issue additional stock in 19x2.

Dividends paid are classified as a financing activity. Exhibit 10.1 shows that Arlen Company paid $10,000 of dividends in 19x2. This amount is shown in Exhibit 10.2.

Generally accepted accounting principles (GAAP) classify other types of cash flows as either investing or financing. The investing category includes both making investments and disposing of investments; for example, the sale of an item of plant is classified as an investing activity, as is the acquisition of an item of plant. Similarly, the financing category includes the repayment of borrowings as well as cash received from loans. Because the cash flow statement shows how each item is classified, users do not need to memorize these GAAP rules.

Thus, an investing activity is not always a cash outflow, and a financing activity is not always a cash inflow.

COMPLETING THE STATEMENT OF CASH FLOWS

We next calculate the increase in cash by summing the three categories in Exhibit 10.2. Note that the $13,000 net increase in cash equals the change in the cash balance as reported on the two balance sheets in Exhibit 10.1.

The cash flow statement shows that although net income was $24,000 in 19x2, Cash increased by only $13,000. Operating activities generated $29,000 in cash. $10,000 of this cash was used to pay dividends. The remaining additional cash inflow was used to acquire new plant. The cost of the new assets was $12,000. $6,000 of this cost was financed by additional borrowing, and cash was used for the remainder. From the cash inflows, $13,000 remained in the Cash account.

USES OF THE STATEMENT OF CASH FLOWS

A forecast of cash flows helps management and other users of financial information to estimate future needs for cash. For example, when a company is growing, the increase in its accounts receivables, inventory, and fixed assets may require more cash. Therefore, although growth may result in additional profits, it may also generate the need for additional cash.

Also, when a company is in financial difficulty, it may pay more attention to its cash flow statement than to its income statement. It pays bills with cash—not net income! Lenders want to know if cash flows are adequate to pay interest on debt and to repay the principal when it becomes due. Similarly, shareholders want to know about the adequacy of cash flow to pay dividends.

A number that it useful for these purposes is called **free cash flow**. It is calculated by subtracting from the cash flow expected from operating activities: (1) the cash needed to purchase normal fixed asset replacements; (2) the cash required to pay long-term debt that is coming due; and (3) normal dividend payments. The difference indicates the amount, if any, that the company is likely to have available: (1) to provide a cushion against unforeseen cash outflows and (2) to provide for discretionary spending; that is, other spending it would like to undertake.

KEY POINTS TO REMEMBER

- A required financial statement, the Statement of Cash Flows, reports the inflows and outflows of cash during the accounting period.

- The statement has three sections: cash flow from operating activities, cash flow from investing activities, and cash flow from financing activities.

- The cash flow from operating activities is found by adjusting net income for (1) changes in current assets and current liabilities and (2) depreciation expense.

- Depreciation expense is not a cash flow. Because it decreases net income, it is added back to net income in order to arrive at the operating cash flow.

- In general, investing activities include the acquisition of new fixed assets and the proceeds of selling fixed assets.

- In general, financing activities include obtaining funds from long term borrowing, repayment of these borrowings, and obtaining funds from issuance of additional stock.

- GAAP has specific requirements for determining which cash flows are classified as investing activities and which are classified as financing activities, but statement users need not memorize these rules because they are evident from the statement itself.

- When a company is growing or when it is experiencing financial crisis, it may pay more attention to the cash flow statement than to the income statement.

PART 11

Analysis of Financial Statements

This part describes:
*   The limitations of financial statement analysis.
*   The nature and limitations of auditing.
*   An approach to analyzing financial statements.
*   Overall measures of performance.
*   Other ratios used in financial statement analysis.

LIMITATIONS OF FINANCIAL STATEMENT ANALYSIS

In this part, we shall describe how information in financial statements is used. Before doing this, let's review the reasons why accounting cannot provide a complete picture of the status or performance of an entity.

One limitation is suggested by the word *financial*; that is, financial statements report only events that can be measured in monetary amounts.

A second limitation is that financial statements are historical; that is, they report only events that *have* happened, whereas we are also interested in estimating events that *will* happen. The fact that an entity earned $1 million last year is not necessarily an indication of what it will earn next year.

Third, the balance sheet does not show the market value of nonmonetary assets. In accordance with the cost concept, plant assets are reported at their unexpired cost. Also, depreciation is a writeoff of cost. It is *not* an indication of changes in the real value of plant assets. The balance sheet does not show the entity's "net worth."

Fourth, the accountant and management have some latitude in choosing among alternative ways of recording an event in the accounts. An example of flexibility in accounting is that in determining inventory values and cost of sales, the entity may use the LIFO, FIFO, or average cost method.

Fifth, many accounting amounts are estimates. In calculating the depreciation expense of a plant asset, for example, one must estimate its service life and its residual value.

AUDITING

All large companies and many small ones have their accounting records examined by independent, certified public accountants. This process is called **auditing**, and the independent accountants are called auditors.

After completing their examination, the auditors write a report giving their opinion. This opinion is reproduced in the company's annual report. A typical opinion is shown in Exhibit 11.1.

Note that the opinion says that the auditors *audited* the financial statements and that these statements are the responsibility of management. The opinion also says that the financial statements *fairly present* the financial results. In the last paragraph of the opinion, the auditors assure the reader that the statements were prepared in conformity with generally accepted accounting principles.

Exhibit 11.1 is an example of a **clean** or **unqualified** opinion. If any of the above statements cannot be made, the auditors call attention to the exceptions in what is called a **qualified** opinion. A qualified opinion can be a serious matter. If the qualification is significant, securities exchanges will immediately suspend trading in the company's stock.

OVERALL MEASURES OF PERFORMANCE

Although they have limitations, financial statements usually are the most useful source of information about an entity. We shall focus first on what they tell about an entity's overall performance.

Equity investors (i.e., shareholders) invest money in a business in order to earn a profit, or **return**, on that equity. Thus, from the viewpoint of the shareholders, the best overall measure of the entity's performance is the return that was earned *on* equity. (This is abbreviated as **ROE**.) The accounting name for the profit or return earned in a year is net income, therefore:

Return on equity is the percentage obtained
by dividing net income by equity.

EXHIBIT 11.1

INDEPENDENT AUDITORS' REPORT

Garsden Company,
its directors and shareholders:

We have audited the balance sheets of Garsden Company as of December 31, 1995 and 1994 and the related income statements and statements of cash flows for each of the three years in the period ended December 31, 1995. These financial statements are the responsibility of the company's management. Our responsibility is to express an opinion on these financial statements based on our audits.

We conducted our audits in accordance with generally accepted auditing standards. These standards require that we plan and perform the audit to obtain reasonable assurance about whether the financial statements are free of material misstatements. An audit includes examining, on a test basis, evidence supporting the amounts and disclosures in the financial statements. An audit also includes assessing the accounting principles used and significant estimates made by management, as well as evaluating the overall financial statement presentation. We believe that our audits provide a reasonable basis for our opinion.

In our opinion, such financial statements present fairly, in all material respects, the financial position of Garsden Company at December 31, 1995 and 1994 and the results of its operations and its cash flows for each of the three years in the period ended December 31, 1995, in conformity with generally accepted accounting principles.

Peane and Burnham

Boston, Massachusetts
February 21, 1996

Example. In 19x2 Arlen Company had net income of $24,000, and its equity on December 31, 19x2 was $130,000. Its ROE for 19x2 was:

$$\frac{\text{Net income}}{\text{Equity}} = \frac{\$24,000}{\$130,000} = 18.5\% \text{ ROE}$$

In order to judge how well Arlen Company performed, its 18.5% ROE must be compared with something. If in 19x1 Arlen Company had an ROE of 20%, we can say that its performance in 19x2 was worse than in 19x1. This is the **historical basis of comparison**.

If in 19x2 another company had an ROE of 15%, Arlen's ROE was better than the other company's. Or, if in 19x2 the average ROE of companies in the same industry as Arlen was 15%, Arlen's ROE was better than the industry average. This is the **external basis of comparison**. If the other company is thought to be the best managed company in the industry, this comparison is called **benchmarking**.

Finally, if from our experience we *judge* that a company like Arlen should have earned an ROE of 20%, we conclude that Arlen's ROE was worse than this **judgmental** standard.

Most comparisons are made in one or more of the following three ways:

1. **Historical**: comparing the entity with its own performance in the past.

2. **External**: comparing the entity with another entity's performance or industry average.

3. **Judgmental**: comparing the entity with a standard based on our judgment.

FACTORS AFFECTING RETURN ON EQUITY

Ratios help explain the factors that influenced return on equity. Some of these were explained in earlier parts. We shall review these ratios and introduce others, using the financial statements of Arlen Company in Exhibit 10.1 and the diagram of these factors in Exhibit 11.2. These ratios are summarized in Exhibit 11.3. We have already described the Return on Equity ratio.

One factor that affects net income is gross margin. In an earlier part, we calculated the **gross margin percentage**. For Arlen Company, this is:

$$\frac{\text{Gross margin}}{\text{Sales revenue}} = \frac{\$120}{\$300} = 40\% \text{ gross margin percentage}$$

EXHIBIT 11.2

ARLEN COMPANY

Factors Affecting Return on Equity

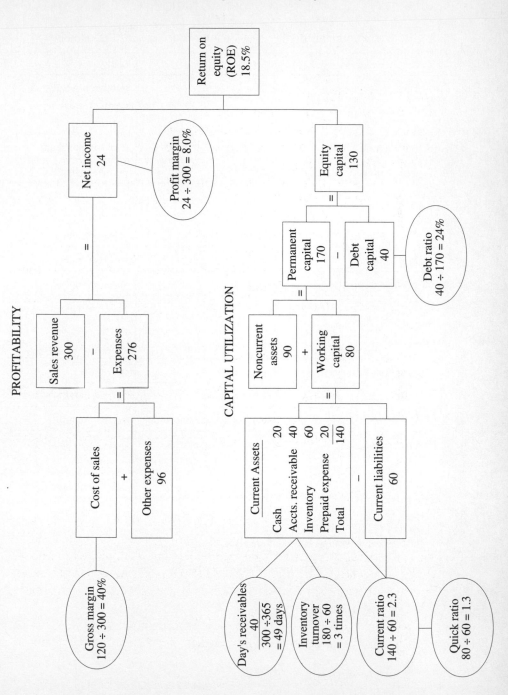

EXHIBIT 11.3

SOME COMMON RATIOS

Overall Performance	Numerator	Denominator
1. Return on equity (ROE)	net income	equity
2. Earnings per share	net income	number of shares of common stock outstanding
3. Price-earnings ratio	average market price	earnings per share
4. Return on permanent capital	EBIT*	permanent capital**
Profitability		
5. Gross margin %	gross margin	sales revenue
6. Profit margin %	net income	sales revenue
7. EBIT margin %	EBIT*	sales revenue
Capital Utilization		
8. Days' receivables	accounts receivable	sales revenue ÷ 365
9. Inventory turnover	cost of sales	inventory
10. Current ratio	current assets	current liabilities
11. Quick ratio	current assets – inventory	current liabilities
12. Debt ratio	noncurrent liabilities	noncurrent liabilities + equity
13. Capital turnover	sales revenue	permanent capital**

* EBIT means Earnings before Interest and Taxes.

** Permanent capital = noncurrent liabilities + equity.

(From here on, when calculating these ratios, we will omit the three zeros to reduce pencil work; that is, we write 120 instead of 120,000.)

Gross margin percentages vary widely. A profitable supermarket may have a gross margin of only 15%. Many manufacturing companies have gross margins of about 35%. Compared with these numbers, the gross margin of Arlen Company is high.

A high gross margin does not necessarily lead to a high net income. Net income is what remains after expenses have been deducted from the gross margin; the higher the expenses, the lower the net income.

The **profit margin percentage** is a useful number for analyzing net income. We calculated it in an earlier part. We calculate it now for Arlen Company:

$$\frac{\text{Net income}}{\text{Sales revenue}} = \frac{\$24}{\$300} = 8\% \text{ profit margin}$$

Statistics on the average profit margin percentage in various industries are published and can be used by Arlen Company as a basis for comparison. Statistics on the average *dollar* amount of net income are not published. Such statistics are not useful because sheer size is not a good indication of profitability.

TESTS OF CAPITAL UTILIZATION

The bottom section of the diagram in Exhibit 11.2 shows the main components of Arlen Company's capital. The information is taken from its balance sheet as of December 31, 19x2. We shall describe ratios that are useful in understanding these components.

As background for this analysis, let's examine some relationships in Camden Company, which has the following condensed balance sheet:

Assets		Liabilities and Equity	
		Total liabilities	$ 400,000
		Total equity	600,000
Total	$1,000,000	Total	$1,000,000

If net income was $60,000, Camden Company's return on equity (ROE) was Net income ÷ Equity, or 10%. If Camden Company could reduce its equity to $500,000, while still maintaining its net income of $60,000, its ROE would become 12%. Thus, with net income held constant, Camden Company can increase its ROE by decreasing its equity.

Since total assets always equal liabilities plus equity, equity can be decreased only if (1) assets are decreased, (2) liabilities are increased, or (3) there is some combination of these two types of changes.

> *Example.* Equity would be decreased by $100,000 (to $500,000) if assets were decreased by $40,000 (to $960,000) and liabilities were increased by $60,000 (to $460,000). If equity was $500,000 and net income was $60,000, ROE would be

$$\frac{\$60}{\$500} = 12\%$$

Thus, in examining how well an entity used its capital, we need to ask two questions:

1. Were assets kept reasonably low?
2. Were liabilities kept reasonably high?

Let's start with the current assets. If current assets are reasonably low in relation to sales volume, this has a favorable effect on ROE.

In earlier parts, two ratios for measuring current assets were described. One related to accounts receivable and was called the **days' receivables ratio**. It shows how many days of sales revenue are tied up in accounts receivable.

Days' receivables for Arlen Company are:

$$\frac{\text{Accounts receivable}}{\text{Sales revenue} \div 365} = \frac{\$40}{\$300 \div 365} = 49 \text{ days}$$

The amount of capital tied up in inventory can be examined by calculating the **inventory turnover ratio**. Since inventory is recorded at cost, this ratio is calculated in relation to cost of sales, rather than to sales revenue.

We can calculate the inventory turnover ratio for Arlen Company as:

$$\frac{\text{Cost of sales}}{\text{Inventory}} = \frac{\$180}{\$60} = 3 \text{ times}$$

If Arlen Company had maintained an inventory of $90,000 to support $180,000 cost of sales, its inventory turnover would have been two times, rather than three times. With this change, its ROE would have been lower than the 18.5% shown in Exhibit 11.2.

The **current ratio** is another way of examining the current section of the balance sheet. In an earlier part we pointed out that if the ratio of current assets to current liabilities is too low, the company might not be able to pay its bills. However, if the current ratio is too high, the company would not be taking advantage of the opportunity to finance current assets with current liabilities. Additional current liabilities would increase its ROE. Equity would inevitably be lower; otherwise, the balance sheet would not balance.

The current ratio for Arlen Company is:

$$\frac{\text{Current assets}}{\text{Current liabilities}} = \frac{\$140}{\$60} = 2.3$$

If Arlen Company decreased its current ratio to 1.5 by increasing its current liabilities, this would increase its ROE. However, such a low current ratio would increase the possibility that Arlen would be unable to pay its current liabilities when they come due.

Caution: The numbers used here to calculate the current ratio are amounts as of the end of the year. Seasonal factors may greatly affect the current ratio during the year. For example, a department store increases its inventory in the fall in anticipation of Christmas business, and its current ratio therefore decreases. Similar limitations affect the other measures discussed in this part.

A variation of the current ratio is the **quick ratio** (also called the **acid-test ratio**). In this ratio, inventory is excluded from the current assets, and the remainder is divided by current liabilities. This is a more stringent measure of bill-paying ability than the current ratio.

The quick ratio for Arlen Company is:

$$\frac{\text{Current assets} - \text{inventory}}{\text{Current liabilities}} = \frac{\$140 - \$60}{\$60} = 1.3$$

The final ratio we shall use in examining capitalization is the **debt ratio**. As explained in Part 9, this is the ratio of debt capital to total permanent capital. Noncurrent liabilities are debt capital, and noncurrent liabilities plus equity is total permanent capital. The debt ratio for Arlen Company is:

$$\frac{\text{Noncurrent liabilities}}{\text{Noncurrent liabilities} + \text{Equity}} = \frac{\$40}{\$40 + \$130} = 24\%$$

The larger the proportion of permanent capital that is obtained from debt, the smaller is the amount of equity capital that is needed. If Arlen had obtained $85,000 of its $170,000 permanent capital from debt, its debt ratio would have been 50%, and its ROE would have been higher than the 18.5% shown in Exhibit 11.2. However, as we learned in Part 9, a high debt ratio results in a more risky capital structure than does a low debt ratio.

In the calculations above, we used balance sheet amounts taken from the ending balance sheet. For some purposes, it is more informative to use an **average** of beginning and ending balance sheet amounts. Arlen Company had $130,000 of equity at the end of 19x2. If it had $116,000 at the beginning of 19x2, its *average* equity during 19x2 was $123,000. Since its net income in 19x2 was $24,000, its return on *average* equity investment was 19.5%.

The return on equity (ROE) in typical American corporations is roughly 15%. Arlen Company's performance in 19x2 was above average.

OTHER MEASURES OF PERFORMANCE

Another measure of performance is **earnings per share**. As the name suggests, the ratio is simply the total earnings (or net income) for a given period divided by the number of shares of common stock outstanding.

Exhibit 10.1 shows that the earnings (i.e., net income) of Arlen Company in 19x2 was $24,000, and that the number of shares outstanding during 19x2 was 4,800. Therefore, earnings per share was $5.

Earnings per share is used in calculating another ratio—the **price-earnings ratio**. It is obtained by dividing the average market price of the stock by the earnings per share. If the average market price for Arlen Company stock during 19x2 was $35, then the price-earnings ratio is the ratio of $35 to $5 or 7 to 1. Price-earnings ratios of many companies are published daily in the financial pages of newspapers. Often, the ratio is roughly 8 to 1, but it varies greatly depending on market conditions. If investors think that earnings per share will increase, this ratio could be much higher. Apparently investors are willing to pay more per dollar of earnings in a growing company.

We have focused on return on equity (ROE) as an overall measure of performance. Another useful measure is the **return on permanent capital**. This shows how well the entity used its capital, without considering how much of its permanent capital came from each of the two sources: debt and equity. This ratio is also called **return on investment (ROI)**.

The *return* portion of this ratio *is not* net income. Net income includes a deduction for interest expense, but interest expense *is* the return on debt capital. Therefore, net income understates the return earned on all permanent capital. Also, income tax expense often is disregarded in order to focus on purely operating activities.

The return used in this calculation is **Earnings Before** the deduction of **Interest** and **Taxes** on income. It is abbreviated as **EBIT**.

As with other income statement numbers, Earnings Before Interest and Taxes (EBIT) is expressed as the percentage of sales revenue. This gives the **EBIT margin**. For Arlen Company this comes to:

$$\frac{\text{EBIT}}{\text{Sales revenue}} = \frac{\$42}{\$300} = 14\% \text{ EBIT margin}$$

The permanent capital as of December 31, 19x2, is the debt capital (i.e., noncurrent liabilities) of $40,000 plus the equity capital of $130,000, a total of $170,000. The return on permanent capital is found by dividing EBIT by this total:

$$\frac{\text{EBIT}}{\text{Permanent capital}} = \frac{\$42}{\$170} = 25\%$$

Another ratio shows how much sales revenue was generated by each dollar of permanent capital. This ratio is called the **capital turnover** ratio. We calculate it for Arlen Company below.

$$\text{Capital turnover} = \frac{\text{Sales revenue}}{\text{Permanent capital}} = \frac{\$300}{\$170} = 1.8 \text{ times}$$

American manufacturing companies have a capital turnover ratio of roughly two times on average. A company that has a large capital investment in relation to its sales revenue is called a **capital-intensive** company. A capital-intensive company, such as a steel manufacturing company or a public utility, has a relatively low capital turnover.

Another way of finding the return on permanent capital is to multiply the EBIT margin by the capital turnover. This relationship can be shown as:

EBIT margin * Capital turnover = Return on permanent capital
14%   *   1.8   =   25%

This formula suggests two fundamental ways in which the profitability of a business can be improved:

1. Increase the EBIT margin.
2. Increase the capital turnover.

Exhibit 11.3 summarizes the ratios discussed in this part.

COMMENTS ON PROFITABILITY MEASUREMENT

In the analysis above, we used ratios because absolute dollar amounts are rarely useful in understanding what has happened in a business. Also, we focused on *both* income and the capital used in earning that income. Focusing on just one of these elements can be misleading.

For example, consider the following results for a supermarket and a department store, each with $10 million of sales revenue.

	Supermarket	Department store
	(000 omitted)	
Sales revenue	$10,000	$10,000
EBIT	400	2,000
Permanent capital	1,000	5,000

The EBIT margin for the supermarket is only $400 \div 10,000 = 4\%$, while for the department store, it is $2,000 \div 10,000 = 20\%$.

However, the department store has more expensive fixtures, a larger inventory, and a lower inventory turnover than the supermarket, so its capital turnover is lower:

	Sales	÷ Permanent Capital	= Capital turnover
Supermarket	$10,000	÷ $1,000	= 10 times
Department store	$10,000	÷ $5,000	= 2 times

The return on permanent capital is the same in both companies, as we can see from the following calculation.

	EBIT margin	* Capital turnover	= Return on permanent capital
Supermarket	0.04	* 10 times	= 40%
Department store	0.20	* 2 times	= 40%

TESTS OF FINANCIAL CONDITION

A business must be concerned with more than profitability. It must also maintain a sound financial condition. This means that it must be able to pay its debts when they come due.

Ability to meet current obligations is called **liquidity**. The current ratio is a widely used measure of liquidity.

Ability to meet long-term obligations is called **solvency**. If a high proportion of permanent capital is obtained from debt, rather than from equity, this increases the danger of insolvency. The proportion of debt is indicated by the debt ratio.

Any of dozens of other ratios may be used for various purposes in analyzing the profitability and financial condition of a business. Those described here are the ones in most general use. Others give a more detailed picture of the important relationships. Financial analysts form their opinions about a company partly by studying ratios such as those we have presented. They also study the details of the financial statements, including the notes that accompany these statements. They obtain additional information by conversations and visits because they realize that the financial statements tell only part of the story about the company.

KEY POINTS TO REMEMBER

- The financial statements do not tell the whole story about an entity because they report only past events, do not report market values, and are based on judgments and estimates. Nevertheless, they provide important information.

- Financial statements are analyzed by using ratios, rather than absolute dollar amounts. These ratios are compared with those for the same entity in the past, with those for similar entities, or with standards based on judgment.

- An overall measure of performance is Return on Equity (ROE). It takes into account both profitability and the capital used in generating profits. Another overall measure is Return on Permanent Capital, or Return on Investment, which is the ratio of profits (adjusted for interest and taxes) to total permanent capital.

- An entity with a low profit margin can provide a good return on equity investment if it has a sufficiently high capital turnover.

- In addition to information about profitability, financial statements provide information about the entity's liquidity and solvency.

Concluding Note

You now know the *essentials* of accounting. There is, of course, much more to the subject. Nevertheless, you now have a basic framework into which you can fit many other transactions when you encounter them. Moreover, notes are added to the financial statements which help explain them and give more detail than the statements themselves. You should always read these notes carefully.

We have used a common set of terms throughout this book. Unfortunately, there is no standard set of terms. Companies can use other terminology. Nevertheless, from your knowledge of the nature of the balance sheet, the income statement, and the statement of cash flows, you can usually figure out what is meant by a term that is not used in this program.

Some transactions are governed by specific rules that are not described in this introductory treatment. For further study, see Robert N. Anthony and James S. Reece, *Accounting Principles*, 7th ed. (Homewood, Illinois: Richard D. Irwin, Inc., 1993).

Glossary

NOTES

1. The explanations are intended as an introduction to the meaning of the terms. They do not encompass all the nuances or qualifications.

2. For a term in *italics*, refer to the entry for that term.

3. If a page number is given, a more complete description of the term will be found beginning on that page.

A

Absorption costing: *Full costing*.

Accelerated depreciation: A method of depreciation that charges off more of the original cost of a plant asset in the earlier years than in the later years of the asset's service life. Used mainly in calculating taxable income. (95)

Account: The record of additions and subtractions for a certain balance sheet or income statement item. (35)

Account payable: The amount that an entity owes to a creditor, usually a supplier, not evidenced by a promissory note. (17)

Account receivable: An amount that is owed to an entity, usually as a result of the ordinary extension of credit to one of its customers. (14)

Accounting: The system for analyzing, recording, summarizing, and reporting the effect of financial events on an entity.

Accounting changes: Material changes (a) in the accounting principles used, (b) in estimates, or (c) in the entity being accounted for. For (a), the cumulative effect of the change is an element of measuring the income of the current period. For (b), the change is recognized in the current and future periods. For (c), both the past and future amounts are affected.

Accounting equation: Assets = Liabilities + Equity. (5)

Accounting income: Income measured according to accounting principles. Contrast with *taxable income*. (70, 99)

Accounting period: The period of time over which an income statement summarizes the changes in equity. Usually the official period is one year, but income statements are also prepared for shorter, or *interim*, periods. (48)

Accounts receivable turnover: A ratio: total credit sales for the year divided by the amount of accounts receivable.

Accretion: An increase in value that results from natural growth, as with timber or nursery stock. Accretion is not usually recognized in financial accounting.

Accrual accounting: Accounting for revenues in the period in which they are earned and for expenses in the period in which they are incurred. This is normal accounting practice. *Cash-basis accounting*, which accounts only for cash receipts and payments, is usually not acceptable. (48)

Accrued expense: An unpaid expense resulting in an *accrued liability*.

Accrued liability: A liability that arises because an expense occurs in a period prior to the related cash payment. Example: Accrued Wages Payable. (64)

Accrued pensions: The amount a company owes its employees for the benefits they accumulated under a pension plan. The liability is measured as the benefits accumulate.

Accumulated depreciation: An account showing the total amount of an asset's depreciation that has been accumulated to date. It is subtracted from the cost of the asset; the difference is the asset's *book value*. (96)

Acid-test ratio: Ratio of monetary current assets to current liabilities. See also *quick ratio*.

Acquisition cost: The price paid, either in cash or equivalent resources, when an asset is acquired. For plant assets, the cost includes all expenditures required to make the asset ready for its intended use. (90)

Actual cost: Amount of resources actually used, as contrasted with *standard cost*, which is an estimate of the amount that should have been used.

Additional paid-in capital: Capital received from shareholders in excess of the par or stated value of the stock that was issued to them. (110)

Adjusting entry: An entry to update the balance originally recorded in an account so that it correctly reflects the revenue or expense of an accounting period and the balance sheet amount as of the end of the period.

Administrative expense: An expense related to the management of the entity as a whole, as contrasted with a functional expense such as production or marketing.

Advances from customers: A liability account showing the amount owed to customers who have paid for goods or services in advance of their delivery. It is sometimes called *deferred revenue*, unearned revenue, or precollected revenue. (52)

Adverse opinion: An external auditor's opinion stating that the financial statements were not presented fairly or were not prepared in accordance with generally accepted accounting principles. Rarely found in practice, however.

Affiliated company: A company that is controlled by another entity.

Aftertax cost: The cost to an entity after the savings in income taxes have been deducted. For example, if the pre-tax interest cost of debt is 12% and the income tax rate is 40%, the aftertax cost is 7.2%.

Agent: A person (including a corporation) authorized to act on behalf of another person. The other person is the principal.

Allocate: To assign a *common cost* to the several *cost objects* that caused it or benefited from it.

Allowance for doubtful accounts: The amount of estimated *bad debts* that is included in accounts receivable. This amount is subtracted from accounts receivable on the balance sheet. (55)

Allowance for funds used during construction: The interest cost associated with *construction work in progress*. The term is used principally by public utilities.

American Institute of Certified Public Accountants (AICPA): The principal association of certified public accountants. AICPA members must adhere to ethical and auditing standards prescribed by the AICPA and to financial accounting standards prescribed by the *FASB*.

Amortization: The process of recognizing the cost of *intangible assets* as expenses. Sometimes the term is used as a general term for writing off long-lived assets of all types. (101)

Annual report: A report prepared by an entity that includes its financial statements, notes to the financial statements, and other material of interest to investors and other outside parties.

Annuity: A series of equal payments made at specified intervals.

Annuity method of depreciation: A method in which the amount of depreciation cost increases in each succeeding year. So named because in an annuity that consists of both principal and interest payments, the amount of principal (which is

similar to depreciation) increases in each succeeding year.

Applied overhead: Overhead costs that are charged to *cost objects*.

Appraised value: The value of an asset that is estimated by an expert, called an appraiser. Contrast this value with that measured by an actual transaction.

Appreciation: An increase in the value of an asset associated with increases in market prices. Contrast this with *accretion*. Appreciation is not recognized in financial accounting.

Arbitrage: The purchase in one market and the simultaneous sale in another market of the identical, or almost identical, security or commodity, in order to make a profit from a difference in prices in the two markets.

Articulate: Said of the relationship between the income statement and the balance sheet. Amounts on the income statement must be reconcilable to changes in amounts on the balance sheet, particularly the change in retained earnings.

Asset: An item of value owned or controlled by the entity that was acquired at a measurable cost. (11)

Asset turnover: A ratio: sales revenue divided by total assets.

Assignment: Transfer of the ownership of an asset, usually accounts receivable, to another party. Contrast this with *pledge*, in which the entity retains ownership of its accounts receivable but uses them as collateral.

Attest: The auditor's function of stating that the financial statements are presented fairly and are prepared in accordance with generally accepted accounting principles.

Auditing: The process of examining the accounting records. The external auditor examines the records as a basis for giving an opinion on the general purpose financial statements. See also *internal audit*. (138)

Auditor's opinion: The statement made by the external auditors as to the fairness of the financial statements and their conformity to generally accepted accounting principles. (138)

Authorized stock: The total number of shares of stock that a corporation is permitted to issue. (The total number actually issued is usually a smaller amount.) (111)

Available for sale: The sum of beginning inventory and purchases during the period. (78)

Average: Although there are several types of averages, the usual meaning in accounting is the arithmetic mean, which is the sum of a set of numbers, divided by the number of items in the set. (146)

Average-cost method: Finding cost of sales by taking the average cost per unit of the beginning inventory plus purchases. (82)

B
Bad debt: An account receivable that never will be collected. (54)

Bad debt expense: The estimated amount of bad debts applicable to an accounting period. (55)

Balance: The difference between the totals of the two sides of an account. An account has either a debit balance or a credit balance. See p. 42 for the procedure for balancing an account.

Balance sheet: A financial statement that reports the assets, liabilities, and equity of a company at one point in time. Assets are listed on the left and liabilities and equity on the right. (11)

Bankrupt: An entity whose liabilities exceed its assets and that has been declared bankrupt by a court. (An excess of liabilities does not, by itself, make an entity bankrupt.)

Basket purchase: The purchase of two or more asset items (e.g., a building and the land it stands on) at a single price. The purchase price subsequently must be divided among these separate assets.

Bearer bond: A bond owned by the person who possesses it. Contrast this with a *registered bond*.

Beginning inventory: The amount of inventory on hand or as recorded in the accounts as of the beginning of the accounting period. (78)

Benchmarking: Comparing an entity's performance with the performance of another company that is thought to be especially well managed. (140)

Betterment: An expenditure for property, plant, or equipment that makes the asset substantially more valuable than the amount originally expended. A betterment is *capitalized*, in contrast to *maintenance* or *repair costs*, which are expensed.

Big bath: Charging unusually large amounts as expenses or losses of the current period, principally by writing down or writing off assets. New managements are sometimes alleged to have authorized a "big bath" in order to reduce the amount of expenses of future periods.

Black, operating in the: Said of an entity whose revenues exceed its expenses.

Bond: A written promise to pay interest and to repay money furnished to the entity, at some future date, usually several years after the date of issue. (107)

Bond discount: The difference between the face value of a bond and the lesser amount received by the entity when the bond is issued. Bond discount must be amortized over the life of the bond issue.

Bond indenture: The agreement between the entity that issues bonds and its bondholders. Usually a lengthy document.

Bond premium: The difference between the face value of a bond and the larger amount received by the entity when the bond is issued. Bond premium must be amortized over the life of the bond issue.

Book inventory: The amount of inventory shown in the accounting records (which may be different from the amount of inventory actually on hand).

Book value: Generally, the amount of an asset recorded in the accounts or the amount of owners' equity recorded in the accounts. For a depreciable asset, this is the difference between its cost and its *accumulated depreciation*. (96)

Boot: The difference between the purchase price of a new asset and the value of an asset traded in. When an entity acquires an asset and trades in another asset as part of the consideration, the additional amount of cash it pays, or agrees to pay, is the boot.

Bottom line: A colloquial term for *net income*.

Breakeven: In general, operating at neither a profit nor a loss. In particular, the volume level at which an entity's income is zero is its breakeven volume.

Burden: An obsolete term for *overhead*.

Business combination: A single entity resulting from the joining together of two or more formerly separate entities. Accounted for as either a *purchase* or a *pooling of interests*.

By-product: A product of relatively low value that results from a production process in which the intention is to produce products of higher value. The other products are called main products.

C

Calendar year: The year that ends on the last day of the calendar, December 31. The accounting period for many entities is the calendar year, but some use a *natural business year*. (48)

Callable bond: A bond that can be paid off at the issuer's option at specified times and specified prices, as stated in the indenture. If the call price exceeds the face value, the excess is the call premium.

Cancelable lease: A lease that can be canceled by the lessee without notice, or on relatively short notice. Contrast this with *capital lease*.

Capacity: The maximum number of units of a product that normally can be produced in a given period of time.

Capital: (1) The amount of owners' equity. (2) The amount of owners' equity plus long-term debt. (3) Long-lived assets. (4) Tangible, long-lived assets. (5) All assets. (Since this word is used with any of several meanings, the meaning in a specific reference must be deduced from the context.)

Capital asset: A long-lived asset, usually a tangible asset.

Capital-intensive: Characterizing a company that has a large capital investment in relation to its sales revenue. (147)

Capital lease: An item an entity controls by a lease agreement that extends over almost the whole life of the item. A capital lease is an asset. (91)

Capital stock: A balance sheet account showing the amount that the shareholder contributed in exchange for stock. Capital stock plus retained earnings equals equity in a corporation. (108)

Capital surplus: An obsolete term for *additional paid-in capital*.

Capital turnover: A ratio: annual sales divided by the amount of *permanent capital.* (147)

Capital utilization, tests of: For a description of these tests, see p. 143.

Capitalize: To record an expenditure as an asset, rather than as an expense of the current period.

Carryback, carryforward: Under certain circumstances, a taxable loss in the current year may be used to recover income taxes paid in earlier years (carryback). Under other circumstances, a taxable loss in the current year may be used to reduce the income tax payment in future years (carryforward).

Carrying cost: The cost associated with holding items in inventory between the time of acquisition and the time of use or delivery to the customer.

Cash: Money, whether in currency or in a bank account. (13)

Cash-basis accounting: An accounting system that does not use the *accrual* basis; it records only cash receipts and payments. It is usually not an acceptable basis for accounting. (48)

Cash discount: A reduction made in the purchase price for a customer who pays within a stated period of time.   .

Cash equivalent: Monetary items which, although not literally cash, can be converted into a known amount of cash in a relatively short period of time. *Certificates of deposit* and *money market funds* are two common types of such items.

Cash flow: Literally, the difference between cash receipts and cash disbursements during a period. In practice, cash flow often is calculated as net income plus depreciation expense. Alternatively, adjustments may be made for any or all of several other "noncash" items. (See Part II.)

Cash flow statement: A financial statement reporting the sources and uses of cash during an accounting period. The cash flow statement, balance sheet, and income statement are the three required financial statements. (121)

Certificate of deposit: The written promise of a bank to pay a specified sum of money on or after a specified date. It is a type of time deposit or cash equivalent.

Certified Public Accountant: A person who has been licensed by a state to practice the profession of public accounting.

Charge; As a verb, to *debit.* As an adjective, a charge customer is a *credit* customer, that is, an account receivable. (Note the possible confusion.)

Charge off: To record as an expense an amount that formerly was recorded as an asset. Usually, the charge is made because the asset no longer has a future benefit.

Chart of accounts: A list of the names and numbers of the accounts included in an accounting system.

CIF: Cost, insurance, and freight. When the term is followed by the name of a port, it indicates that the price includes these items up to the delivery at that port.

Circulating capital: *Working capital.*

Claim: Amount owed to creditors or others who have provided money or have extended credit to a business.

Clean opinion: An external auditor's report that contains no qualifications. (138)

Clearing account: An account used in the closing process to accumulate temporarily items that enter into the calculation of income statement categories.

Closing entries: Journal entries that transfer the balances in revenue and expense accounts for a period to *retained earnings.* (41)

Coinsurance: A requirement in many property insurance policies requiring that if the insured amount is not at least a specified percentage of the value of the property, the owner will not collect the full amount of insurance in the event of loss.

COLA: Cost of living adjustment. An automatic change (usually an increase) in wage or salary rates when the cost of living changes by a specified percentage; an element of many labor contracts.

Collateral: Assets pledged by a borrower.

Commercial paper: Notes payable issued by corporate borrowers as evidence of the amount borrowed. Commercial paper usually is issued only by corporations with high credit ratings.

Common costs: Costs that are applicable to two or more cost objects and that must be *allocated* to these cost objects.

Common stock: Stock, the owners of which are not entitled to preferential treatment with regard to dividends or to the distribution of assets in the event of liquidation. Its book value is not related to its market value. (110)

Common stock equivalent: A security or option, the value of which is closely related to the value of the corporation's common stock because it is convertible into common stock at the holder's option.

Comparisons, bases of: Performance compared with past performance, with performance of other entities, or with a judgmental standard. (140)

Compensating balance: An amount that a bank requires a borrower to maintain on deposit as a condition of a loan. Entities must disclose the amount of significant compensating balances.

Completed contract method: Revenue is recognized only when the contract has been completed. Permitted for long-term contracts only if the amount of income cannot be reliably estimated at the end of each accounting period. Contrast this method with the *percentage-of-completion method.*

Composite depreciation: A single depreciation calculation applied to a group of assets, even though the assets are dissimilar. (If similar, the calculation would be *group depreciation.*)

Compound interest: Interest calculated on the principal plus the amount of previously accumulated interest. Contrast this with *simple interest.*

Compound interest method of depreciation: A method of depreciation that has essentially the same effect as the *annuity method of depreciation.*

Comprehensive income: The net effect of all changes in owners' equity during an accounting period other than those associated with transactions with owners. This is discussed in "FASB Concepts Statement 3."

Comptroller: Obsolete spelling of *controller.* The word is pronounced as controller, despite the spelling.

Concepts: See p. 72 for a summary of accounting concepts.

Conglomerate: An entity that engages in several dissimilar lines of business.

Conservatism concept: Recognize increases in equity only when they are reasonably certain; recognize decreases as soon as they are reasonably possible. (49)

Consignment: Goods held for sale by a retailer but owned by the manufacturer or distributor. The person holding the goods is the consignee. The owner of the goods is the consignor.

Consistency: Accounting for transactions of a similar type in the same way from one period to the next. This does not mean that dissimilar transactions are accounted for in the same way. For example, the fact that inventory is adjusted downward to market value, whereas plant assets are not so adjusted, is not inconsistent.

Consolidated financial statements: Financial statements prepared for a corporate family as an entity. The family consists of a parent and those subsidiaries in which the parent owns more than 50% of the stock. (117)

Constant dollar accounting: A supplementary system of financial statements in which amounts are stated in dollars of constant purchasing power.

Construction Work in Progress (CWIP): An inventory account used to report costs incurred to date for the construction of new plant.

Contingency: An amount that may become a liability under conditions that may occur in the future. If probable and if the amount can be estimated, a liability is recognized; otherwise, a material contingency is disclosed in the notes to the financial statements but is not stated as a liability.

Continuing operations: Operations of the current period that are expected to continue in the future. Revenues and expenses are reported separately from those of *discontinued operations*.

Contra account: An account that accumulates amounts that are in fact subtractions from another account. An example is Accumulated Depreciation, which is a deduction from the asset account, Plant. (96)

Contra asset: A *contra account* to an asset account. For example, Allowance for Doubtful Accounts is a contra account to Accounts Receivable. (55, 96)

Contributed capital: The sum of the *par* or *stated value* of stock plus the amount of other paid-in capital. Does *not* refer to *donated capital*.

Contribution margin: The difference between revenue and *variable costs*.

Contributory pension plan: A pension plan in which some or all contributions are made by the employees.

Controllable cost: An element of cost, the amount of which can be influenced by a manager. (The manager does not necessarily have complete control over the cost.)

Controller: The person responsible for operating an entity's accounting system and often other information systems; may be the chief financial officer.

Conversion cost: The labor and overhead cost of converting raw material into finished products. (84)

Convertible bond: A bond that can be converted into a specified amount of stock at the holder's option.

Convertible preferred stock: *Preferred stock* that can be converted into a specified amount of *common stock* at the holder's option.

Copyright: The right to the exclusive use of a book, play, article, or other material granted by the government to its author and the author's assignees for a period of his or her life plus 50 years.

Corporation: A legal entity, with most of the rights and obligations of an individual person. The rights are granted by a state.

Cost: A monetary measure of the amount of resources used for some purpose. See also *product cost, acquisition cost*, and *period costs*.

Cost accounting: The process of identifying and accumulating manufacturing costs and assigning them to goods in the manufacturing process. (84)

Cost center: An accounting device used for the accumulation of the costs of a process, organization unit, or other cost object.

Cost concept: Accounting focuses on the original cost of assets, rather than on their market value. (10)

Cost object: Any product, process, or organization unit for which costs are accumulated.

Cost of capital: The cost of using debt and equity capital; interest.

Cost of goods manufactured: The total cost of goods for which manufacture was completed during an accounting period. Contrast this with *manufacturing costs*, which are the costs incurred in the manufacturing process during the period, whether or not the goods were completed.

Cost of sales: The cost of the same products whose revenues are included in sales revenue. For merchandise, the label often used is cost of goods sold. (75)

Credit: (1) As a noun, the right-hand side of an account or an amount entered on the right-hand side. (2) As a verb, to make an entry on the right-hand side of an account. Rules for debit and credit are summarized on pp. 39 and 40. (3) Permission to pay a bill subsequent to the purchase date; also, the amount of such a bill.

Creditor: A party who lends money or extends credit to an entity. (3)

Cumulative preferred stock: *Preferred stock*, dividends for which accumulate if not paid currently. Usually, cumulative dividends must be paid before any dividends can be paid to common shareholders.

Current assets: Cash and assets that are expected to be converted into cash or used up in the near future, usually within one year. (13)

Current liabilities: Obligations that become due within a short period of time, usually one year. (16)

Current ratio: The ratio obtained by dividing the total of current assets by the total of current liabilities. (17, 145)

Current value accounting: Amounts reported in a system of supplementary financial statements in which assets are stated at their current values, rather than at actual costs less depreciation. Rarely used in published financial statements.

D

Days' receivables: The number of days of sales that are tied up in accounts receivable as of the end of an accounting period. Sales per day is found by dividing annual credit sales by 365, and accounts receivable is divided by sales per day to find the days' receivables. (56)

Debit: (1) As a noun, the left-hand side of an account or an amount entered on the left-hand side. (2) As a verb, to make an entry on the left-hand side of an account. (39)

Debt: An amount owed by an entity, usually evidenced by a document and usually with a specified payment date.

Debt capital: Capital raised by the issuance of debt securities, usually bonds. (107) For differences between debt capital and *equity capital*, see p. 107.

Debt ratio: The ratio of *debt capital* to total *permanent capital*. A measure of an entity's financial risk. (116, 145)

Debtor: A party who owes money to an entity.

Declining balance depreciation: A method in which the depreciation expense is calculated as a constant percentage of the asset's book value. Usually, the percentage is double the straight-line percentage.

Deduction method: Finding cost of sales by adding the beginning inventory and purchases and subtracting the ending inventory. (77)

Default: Failure to pay interest or principal on debt when due.

Deferred charge: An expenditure that is recorded as an asset until the period in which the benefits are received.

Deferred income taxes: The difference between actual income taxes for the period and income tax expense. (100)

Deferred revenue: Used to mean, but less desirable than, *advances from customers*.

Deficit: Negative retained earnings.

Defined-benefit plan: A pension plan in which the employer promises to pay specified amounts to eligible employees.

Defined-contribution plan: A pension plan in which contributions by or on behalf of each employee are specified. Pension payments are based on the annuity that could be purchased with such contributions.

Demand deposit: Money in a checking account in a bank.

Depletion: The process of recognizing as expense the cost of a wasting asset, such as natural gas, coal, oil, or other minerals. (101)

Depreciable cost: The difference between the cost of a long-lived asset and its estimated *residual value*. (93)

Depreciation expense: The portion of the estimated net cost of plant assets (e.g., buildings, equipment) that becomes an expense in a given accounting period. (63, 92) For accounting entries, see p. 96. For depreciation in calculating taxable income, see p. 99. For depreciation in calculating cash provided by operations, see p. 125.

Depreciation rate: The percentage of the cost of an asset that is an expense each year. In the straight-line method, the rate is 1 divided by the *service life*. (94)

Dilution: A possible reduction in earnings per share that would result if stock *options* or *warrants* were exercised or convertible securities were converted to stock.

Direct cost: A cost element assigned to a single *cost object*. Direct costs include direct materials, direct labor, and, in some circumstances, direct services. Contrast this with *indirect cost*, which is a cost element allocated to several cost objects.

Disbursement: Payment of cash. Contrast this with *expenditure*.

Disclaimer of opinion: A report in which an external auditor states that an opinion on the fairness of the financial statements cannot be given.

Disclosure: Reporting information in the financial statements, including the notes thereto.

Discontinued operations: A division or other segment of an entity that has been identified as being for sale or which otherwise will no longer be a part of the entity. The gain or loss on disposition, after deducting related income taxes, and the *income from discontinued operations* are reported on the income statement separately from continuing operations.

Discount: Any deduction from a gross amount. A bond discount is the difference between the face amount of the bond and its market value. A sales discount is a deduction from the selling price for prompt payment or other reasons. It is the opposite of *premium*.

Disposition of plant, gain or **loss on:** The difference between *book value* and the amount actually realized from the sale of a plant asset. (98)

Dividend: The funds generated by profitable operations that are distributed to shareholders. Dividends are *not* an expense. (70, 112)

Dividend yield: A ratio: the dividend paid in a year on a share of stock divided by the market price of the stock.

Donated capital: Equity provided by persons who do not expect a return on their equity. It is usually limited to endowment of or other contributions to nonprofit organizations.

Double-declining balance depreciation: A form of *declining balance depreciation* in which the percentage applied to the book value is double the straight-line depreciation rate.

Double-entry system: A fundamental characteristic of accounting. Each transaction causes at least two changes in the accounts. (23)

Dual-aspect concept: The total assets of an entity always are equal to its total liabilities + equity. (4)

E

Earned surplus: An obsolete term, referring to *retained earnings*.

Earnings: Another term for *net income*.

Earnings before interest and taxes (EBIT): An amount used in calculating return on *permanent capital*. (147)

Earnings per share: A ratio: total earnings for a given period divided by the equivalent number of shares of common stock outstanding. (146)

Earnings, retained: See *Retained earnings*.

Economic life: The period over which an asset is expected to provide benefits to an entity. It is the same as *service life*.

Ending inventory: The amount of inventory on hand as of the end of an accounting period.

Entity: A business concern or other organization for which a set of accounts is kept. (6)

Entity concept: Business accounts are kept for entities, rather than for the persons who own, operate, or are otherwise associated with those entities. (6)

Entry: The accounting record made for a single transaction. (42)

EPS: Earnings per share.

Equation, fundamental accounting: Assets = Liabilities + Equity.

Equity: Capital supplied by (1) equity investors and (2) the entity's retained earnings. In an unincorporated entity, the category is called owners' equity, or capital; in a corporation, the category is called shareholders' equity. The category is also known as claims against the entity by equity investors. (Less common, the category indicates all the items on the right-hand side of the balance sheet, that is, the sum of liabilities plus owners' equity.) (108)

Equity capital: The capital supplied by equity investors. (108) For differences between debt and equity capital, see p. 114.

Equity method: A method of accounting for one entity's investment in another entity. In this method, a record is kept of the share of the entity's equity that is represented by the investment. Contrast this with the consolidation method, in which the other entity's assets and liabilities are combined with those of the reporting entity.

Equity ratio: Shareholder equity divided by total *permanent capital*.

Estimated tax liability: The amount owed to the government for taxes. (17, 100)

Exchange rate: The price of one country's currency stated in terms of another country's currency.

Excise tax: A tax on the manufacture, sale, or consumption of goods or services.

Expenditure: The decrease in an asset or increase in a liability associated with the acquisition of goods or services. Do not confuse expenditure with *expense*, which represents the use of goods and services and which may occur after the expenditure. (60)

Expense: A decrease in equity associated with activities of an accounting period; that is, resources used up or consumed during an accounting period. Example: wage expense. (60) For assets that will become expenses, see pp. 60 and 62; for expenses that create liabilities, see p. 64. Dividends are *not* an expense, however.

Expensing: The process of charging the cost of an asset to expense.

Expired cost: Another name for expense. (62)

External basis of comparison: Comparing an entity's performance with the performance of other entities. (140)

Extraordinary gain (loss): A large, unusual, and infrequent gain or loss.

F

Face amount: The total amount of a loan that must be repaid; it is specified on the face of a bond. (107)

Factoring: Selling notes receivable or accounts receivable to another party (the factor) at a discount, in order to obtain cash.

Factory burden: An obsolete term for *production overhead cost*.

Fair value: The price that was, or would be, paid in an arm's length exchange between two parties, both of whom have all available information about the item being exchanged.

FASB: Financial Accounting Standards Board, the body designated to produce financial accounting standards for nongovernmental entities.

Federal Insurance Contributions Act (FICA): Specifies the amount of contributions for Social Security. FICA is an abbreviation used to designate these amounts.

Federal Unemployment Tax Act: Specifies unemployment compensation taxes. FUTA is an abbreviation referring to these taxes.

FIFO (First-In, First-Out) method: Finding the cost of sales, using the assumption that the oldest goods (those first in) were the first to be sold (first out). (81)

Financial accounting income: income measured according to accounting principles. (70, 99)

Financial statements: See the three required financial statements: balance sheet, income statement, cash flow statement.

Financing lease: The name used in the accounts of a lessor for *capital lease*.

Finished goods inventory: Goods that have been completely manufactured but not yet shipped.

Fiscal year: *Accounting period*, *natural business year*. (48)

Fixed asset: Tangible, noncurrent assets; property, plant, and equipment. (90)

Fixed cost: A cost element that does not vary with the volume of activity.

Float: The amount of outstanding checks; that is, checks that have been drawn but not yet received and paid by the entity's bank.

Flow report: A report of flows during a period of time, such as an income statement or a cash flow statement. (32)

FOB: Free on board at a specified location. The seller or shipper pays transportation costs to this location.

Foreign exchange gain (loss): The gain (loss) from holding net foreign monetary items during a period, resulting from a change in the exchange rate.

Franchise: A right to use another entity's trade name or to sell its products or services.

Free cash flow: An approximation of the amount of cash a company is likely to have available to meet unforeseen needs and to provide discretionary spending. For the calculation of free cash flow, see p. 134.

Freight-In: The transportation cost of goods purchased. Conceptually, it should be added to the cost of the goods, but often freight-in is treated as a separate expense element.

Fringe benefits: Benefits, principally monetary, beyond *wages*; owed to an employee because of his or her service to the company. (64)

Full cost: The direct cost of a cost object plus a fair share of its *indirect cost*. Contrast this with *direct cost*.

Full cost method: A method used in extractive industries (oil, gas) in which most exploration costs are capitalized.

Full costing: Determining the full cost of a cost object.

Fully diluted earnings per share: The lowest earnings-per-share amount for common stock, obtained by assuming that all stock *options* and *warrants* are exercised and all convertible securities have been converted. It must be reported on the income statement.

Fund: See *funds*.

Funded: Refers to a pension plan in which funds have been set aside to meet the estimated pension obligations. Most pension plans are funded to some extent, but some

are not *fully funded*; that is, the amount of the fund is not equal to the estimated obligation.

Funds: An ambiguous term, sometimes referring to *working capital*, sometimes to the monetary components of working capital, and sometimes to cash. The intended meaning must be determined from the context.

Funds provided by operations: Another term for cash flow from operating activities. A category on a cash flow statement, usually referring to net income plus depreciation expense, deferred income taxes, and other items not requiring the use of working capital or cash. (122)

G

Gain: The excess of the amount over the *book value* of an asset that was realized from the sale of assets such as property, plant, equipment, or securities (but not merchandise). (98)

General expenses: Expenses other than cost of sales, selling expenses, and (in some entities) interest expense and administrative expense.

General purpose financial statements: Financial statements prepared for the use of investors and other outside parties. These statements must be prepared in accordance with *generally accepted accounting principles* (GAAP). Contrast this with financial statements prepared for management, to which GAAP need not apply.

Generally accepted accounting principles (GAAP): Principles (often called *standards*) stated by the Financial Accounting Standards Board and its predecessors, and other principles that are accepted because they are widely used.

Going-concern concept: The accounting concept that assumes that a business will continue to operate indefinitely. (9)

Goods: Tangible products, usually intended for sale. Products consist of goods and *services*.

Goods available for sale: The sum of the beginning inventory plus purchases during the period. (78)

Goods in process: *Work in process inventory.*

Goodwill: An intangible asset; the amount paid in excess of the value of a company's identifiable net assets, representing an amount paid for a favorable location or reputation. Goodwill is recognized as an asset only if it was purchased. (16)

Grandfather clause: A clause in an accounting standard that exempts transactions entered into prior to a specified date from the new standard.

Gross: An amount before deductions. Gross sales revenue is revenue before deductions of sales discounts, returns, and allowances.

Gross margin: The difference between sales revenue and *cost of sales*. (70)

Gross margin percentage: Gross margin as a percentage of sales revenue. (140)

Gross profit: *Gross margin.*

Group depreciation: A depreciation method in which similar items are grouped together and depreciation expense is calculated on the group as a whole, rather than on individual items. (*Composite depreciation* refers to this calculation for dissimilar items.)

H
Half-year convention: Taking half a year's depreciation in the year an asset was acquired.

Historical basis of comparison: Comparing an entity's performance with its own performance in the past. (140)

Historical cost: The cost actually incurred for an asset at the time the asset was acquired. Accounting principles generally trace the historical cost of assets, rather than their current value.

Holding gain (loss): The gain (loss) incurred from holding assets during an accounting period because of a change in their current value. Holding gains are not recognized in accounting. Holding losses are recognized for inventory and marketable securities, under certain circumstances, but not for other assets.

I
Identifiable asset: In segment reporting, an asset that is specifically traced to a segment. In acquisitions, an asset, other than goodwill, that was owned by the entity being acquired.

Imprest fund: A fund, usually for petty cash, which is maintained at a predetermined amount, represented by cash on hand plus receipted bills for amounts paid out.

Improvement: An expenditure that extends the useful life of an asset or increases the functions that it performs beyond the life or function of the asset at the time it was acquired. An improvement is capitalized. Contrast this with *maintenance* or *repair cost*.

Imputed cost: A cost that, although real, is not recorded in the accounting records.

Income: The difference between revenue and expense. *Net income* is the difference between all revenues and all expenses. *Operating income* is the difference between revenues and operating expenses. (30, 70)

Income from continuing operations: Revenues less expenses, except for those relating to *discontinued operations* and *extraordinary* items, and also excluding the effect of changes in accounting principles.

Income from discontinued operations: The income, after allowance for income taxes, from major activities of an entity that have been discontinued during the period or from major activities for which a decision to discontinue them has been made.

Income statement: A statement of revenues and expenses, and the difference between them, for an accounting period; a flow report. It explains the changes in equity associated with operations of the period. (30) See p. 70 for income statement format.

Income summary: A temporary ledger account used to calculate net income.

Income tax: A tax that is levied as a percentage of *taxable income*. (99)

Indenture: *Bond indenture*.

Indexing: Adjusting a payment so that it varies with the amount of inflation. For example, a cost-of-living adjustment (*COLA*) is indexing of employees' earnings.

Indirect cost: A cost element that relates to more than one *cost object*. In accounting for *full costs*, a fair share of the cost is allocated to each cost object.

Inflation accounting: Accounting that reflects the effect of inflation. It is reported as supplementary information by some entities, but is never included in the primary financial statements. See *constant dollar accounting*, *current value accounting*.

Insolvent: An entity that is unable to pay its debts when they are due. When a court recognizes that the entity is insolvent, the entity is *bankrupt*.

Installment: Payment of a debt or an account receivable in several amounts at periodic intervals, rather than in one sum.

Installment method: A method of recognizing income on installment sales. For each installment, expenses are recognized in proportion to the fraction of the selling price that is collected. This method is permitted for income tax accounting. For financial accounting, it is permitted only if the collection of installments is highly uncertain.

Intangible asset: An asset that has no physical substance, such as *goodwill* or the protection provided by an insurance policy. (16)

Intercompany transactions: Transactions between the corporations in a consolidated family. These transactions are eliminated in preparing *consolidated financial statements*. (117)

Interest: The cost incurred for the use of money.

Interest expense: The entity's cost of using borrowed funds during an accounting period.

Interest revenue: Revenue earned from permitting another party to use an entity's money; revenue from the "rental" of money. It is often, but erroneously, called interest income. (54)

Interim statements: Financial statements prepared for a period shorter than one year, such as a month or a quarter. (48)

Internal audit: An audit conducted by an entity's employees, as contrasted to an external audit conducted by independent auditors.

Internal Revenue Service (IRS): An agency of the U.S. Treasury Department responsible for writing income tax regulations in accordance with the Internal Revenue Code (which is enacted by the Congress), and for collecting income and other taxes.

Intrafamily transaction: *Intercompany transactions.*

Inventory (noun): Goods being held for sale, raw materials, and partially finished products. (75) For inventory valuation methods, see p. 79. For write-down to market, see p. 83.

Inventory (verb): To conduct a physical count of inventory.

Inventory turnover: A ratio: cost of sales divided by average inventory. It shows how many times inventory was totally replaced during the year. (86, 144)

Investment tax credit: A reduction in income tax liability, calculated as a percentage of the cost of newly purchased long-lived assets (with certain exceptions).

Investments: Securities that are held for a relatively long period of time and are purchased for reasons other than the temporary use of excess cash. They are noncurrent assets.

Invoice: A document prepared by the seller describing the items sold and the amount the buyer owes for them.

Issue: As a verb, to exchange stock for cash or other valuable consideration. An entity *issues* its stock; it does not sell its own stock. Stockholders *sell* their stock to others.

Issued stock: The shares of stock that have been issued. Issued stock less *treasury stock* equals *outstanding stock*. (111) Contrast with *authorized stock.*

J

Job-order costing: A system of cost accounting in which costs are accumulated for individual jobs. Contrast this with *process costing.*

Joint cost: A cost that is caused by the production of two or more products. A

fair share of the cost is allocated to each product.

Journal: A record in which transactions are recorded in chronological order. It shows the accounts to be debited or credited and the amount of each debit and credit. (41)

Journal entry: *Entry.*

Judgmental basis of comparison: Comparing an entity's performance with personal judgment. (140)

L

Labor: Services provided by an entity's employees. It is distinguished from purchased services, which are provided by external parties.

Land: Real property, other than buildings. Land usually is assumed to have an indefinitely long life and hence is not depreciated. (91)

Lease: An agreement under which the owner of property permits someone else to use it. The owner is the lessor. The user is the lessee. (90)

Leasehold improvement: An asset representing expenditures to improve leased property. The improvement should be amortized over the life of the lease or the life of the improvement, whichever is shorter.

Ledger: A group of accounts. Entries are posted to the ledger from the *journal.* (41)

Leverage: The proportion of *debt capital* to *total permanent capital.* (106)

Liability: The claim of a creditor. (15)

LIFO (Last-In, FIrst-Out) method: Finding the cost of sales, using the assumption that the goods most recently purchased (those last in) were the first to be sold (first out). (81)

Limitations on financial statement analysis: For a description of these limitations, see p. 137.

Line of credit: An agreement with a financial institution in which it agrees to loan money to an entity on demand, up to a specified limit and for a specified (usually short) period of time.

Liquid asset: Cash or an asset that can quickly be turned into cash, such as marketable securities and, in some cases, accounts receivable.

Liquidation value: The amount that creditors or shareholders are supposed to receive if the corporation is dissolved. For shareholders, this refers primarily to *preferred stock* since common shareholders cannot be promised a specified amount.

Liquidity: An entity's ability to meet its current obligations, often measured by the *current ratio*. (149)

Long-lived asset: An asset with a service life of two or more accounting periods, and hence a noncurrent asset; property, plant, and equipment. (A few assets, such as multi-year insurance policies, are often classified as current, as an exception to this rule.) (89)

Loss: An expense resulting from an asset, the future benefit of which has expired during a period (for example, from fire or theft) or from a liability that was incurred without a debit to an asset occurring in a period (for example, from lawsuits). See also *gain*. The FASB classifies a loss as a separate element, rather than as a type of expense. (66)

Lower of cost or market: The accounting rule for valuing inventory and marketable equity securities. The amount reported is the lower of acquisition cost and net realizable value (estimated selling price less selling costs).

M

Maintenance: Expenditures incurred to keep a plant asset in good condition. These expenditures are costs of the current period, in contrast to *improvements*, which are capitalized.

Manufacturing company: A company that converts raw materials into finished, salable products and sells these products. For accounting for inventory in a manufacturing company, see p. 83.

Manufacturing costs: Costs incurred in the manufacturing process during an accounting period, whether or not the goods were completed.

Manufacturing overhead (or expense): *Production overhead cost.*

Margin: The difference between revenue and specified expenses.

Marginal cost: *Direct cost.*

Market value: The amount for which an asset can be sold in the marketplace. (10)

Marketable securities: Securities that are expected to be converted into cash within a year; a current asset. (14)

Markon: The relation between cost and selling price of a product. The term *markup* is also used, sometimes as a synonym and other times for a different relationship. For example, a markon (or markup) of 40% can mean that the selling price is 140% of the cost, or it can mean the cost is 60% of the selling price.

Matching concept: When a given transaction has both a revenue element and an expense element (such as *cost of sales*), both elements should be reported in the same accounting period. (62) For matching of income tax expenses, see p. 100.

Materiality concept: Disregard trivial matters; disclose all important matters. (50)

Merchandising company: A company that sells goods it has acquired from other businesses; for example, a retail store or a wholesaler. (83)

Merger: The joining together of two or more entities. Usually, one entity acquires the other. See *business combination*.

Minority interest: The equity of those shareholders in a subsidiary other than the equity of the parent. This is reported as an equity item on the consolidated balance sheet. (118)

Modified Accelerated Cost Recovery System: The Internal Revenue Service system of *accelerated depreciation* for plant assets, ordinarily used in calculating taxable income. Assets are classified as having 3-year, 5-year, or 10-year lives, and specified percentages of cost are allowed for each year in each class. (99)

Monetary assets: Cash and promises by an outside party to pay the business a specified amount of money. (56)

Monetary liabilities: Liabilities in which the obligation is to pay a specified amount of money.

Money market fund: A mutual fund consisting of short-term, readily marketable securities.

Money-measurement concept: Accounting records report only facts that can be expressed in monetary terms. Accounting therefore does not give a complete record of an entity. (5)

Mortgage: A pledge of real estate as security for a loan. (26)

Mortgage payable: The liability for a loan that is secured by a mortgage. (26)

N

Natural business year: A year that ends on a day in the period in which activities are at a relatively low level. For some enti-ties, the accounting period is the natural business year (also called the fiscal year), rather than the calendar year. (48)

Negotiable instrument: An instrument that is readily transferable to another party.

Net: The amount remaining after something has been subtracted from a *gross* amount. Example: accounts receivable, net.

Net assets: (1) Used by the *FASB* to mean total assets minus liabilities (which is the same as equity). (2) Used by the financial community to mean working capital plus noncurrent assets.

Net current assets: A less desirable term for *working capital*.

Net income: The amount by which total revenues exceed total expenses for an accounting period; the "bottom line." (70)

Net income percentage: A ratio: net income divided by sales revenue. (72)

Net loss: Negative net income.

Net realizable value: The current market value of an item less the cost of selling it.

Net sales revenue: Gross sales revenue less cash discounts, returns, and allowances.

Net worth: A commonly used, but misleading, term for *equity*.

Nominal account: A revenue or expense account. It is nominal because it is closed into retained earnings at the end of the period. Contrast this with *real account*.

Nonbusiness organization: Municipalities, hospitals, religious organizations, and other organizations that are not operated for the purpose of earning a profit. (7)

Noncancelable lease: A lease that cannot be canceled by either party for a specified period of time. If the period approximates the service life of the asset, the lessee accounts for such a lease as a *capital lease* and the lessor accounts for it as a *financing lease*.

Noncontributory pension plan: A pension plan in which all contributions are made by the employer and none by the employees.

Noncurrent asset: An asset that is expected to be of use to the entity for longer than one year. (15, 89)

Noncurrent liability: A claim that does not fall due within one year; similar to *debt capital*. (17, 107)

Nonprofit organization: An organization whose profits cannot be distributed to owners. Various types of nonprofit organizations are defined in Section 501 of the Internal Revenue Code. Although government entities fit the definition, some people place government entities in a separate category.

No-par-value stock: Common stock that does not have a predetermined par value. It is recorded at its *stated value*. (111)

Note: A written promise to pay.

Note payable: A liability of an entity, evidenced by a *promissory note*. (16)

Note receivable: An amount owed to an entity, evidenced by a *promissory note*. (14)

O

Obsolescence: A loss in the usefulness of an asset because of the development of improved equipment, changes in style, or other causes not related to the physical condition of the asset. It is one cause of depreciation; the other is the wearing out of an asset. (92)

OPEB: *Other Post-Employment Benefits.*

Operating expenses: Expenses associated with operating activities. (70)

Operating income: The difference between revenues and operating expenses.

Operating lease: Any lease that is not a *capital lease*. Lease costs are accounted for as costs or expenses of the current period. The term rental is often used to refer to the cost of an operating lease.

Operations: An imprecise term for an entity's principal activities.

Opinion: The report in which the external auditor states an opinion as to the fairness of the financial statements. (138)

Option: The right to buy something at a specified price during a specified period of time.

Organization costs: The costs of organizing an entity and getting it ready to function. Although these costs can be capitalized under certain circumstances, they often are charged as expenses of the first period in which the entity has revenues.

Other assets: Noncurrent assets other than property, plant, and equipment; usually intangible. (15)

Other paid-in capital: The amount paid by investors in excess of the *par* or *stated value* of the stock. (110)

Other post-employment benefits: Health care or other *fringe benefits*, besides pensions, owed to an employee after his or her employment ends. (65)

Outlay: *Disbursement.*

Out-of-pocket cost: A cost that requires the use of cash, either immediately or in the near future.

Outstanding stock: Shares of stock held by investors. It consists of *issued stock* less *treasury stock*. (111)

Overhead cost: *Production overhead cost.*

Overhead rate: A rate used to allocate overhead costs to products. (85)

Owners' equity: The interest of owners in the assets of a business. In a corporation, owners' equity consists of capital stock plus retained earnings. (108) The word *equity* has the same meaning.

P

Package of accounting reports: A balance sheet at the beginning of an accounting period, another at the end of the period, and an income statement for the period. (70)

Paid-in capital: The amount paid by investors in exchange for stock. The amount in excess of the stock's *par* or *stated value* is called other paid-in capital. (18, 110)

Par value: The specific amount printed on the face of some stock certificates. It is no longer significant in accounting. (110)

Parent: A corporation that controls one or more other corporations because it owns more than 50 percent of their stock. The controlled corporations are its *subsidiaries*. (117)

Participating preferred stock: Preferred stock that is entitled to a minimum stated dividend plus an additional dividend to be paid if common dividends exceed a specified amount.

Partnership: An unincorporated business with two or more owners. (109)

Past-service cost: The part of the cost of a pension plan that relates to services performed by employees prior to the inception of the plan.

Patent: A right granted by the federal government to exclude others from profiting from an invention of a product or process for a period of 17 years. If the entity pur-chased the patent, it is an asset. If the patent was developed internally, the cost of developing it is an expense.

Payout ratio: Common stock dividends declared in a year divided by the net income for the year.

P-E ratio: *Price-earnings ratio.*

Pension fund: A fund that provides an annuity to retired employees. Usually the pension fund is held by an outside trustee; if so, it is not an asset of the entity.

Per books: An amount shown in the accounting records.

Percent: A number obtained by dividing one number by another (which is the base, or 100 percent), and multiplying by 100. Income statement items are often expressed as percentages of sales revenue. (72)

Percentage-of-completion method: A method of recognizing revenue on a construction contract (or similar contract that requires a long time to complete). The revenue for a period is in proportion to the percentage of the contract that was completed in that period.

Performance, measures of: For overall measures of performance, see p. 138; for tests of capital utilization, see p. 143; for other measures, see p. 146.

Period: *Accounting period.*

Period costs (or expenses): Costs associated with general sales and administrative activities. Contrast this with *product costs*. (84)

Permanent account: An account for a balance sheet item, so called because it is not closed at the end of the accounting period. Contrast this with *temporary account*. (44)

Permanent capital: The sum of noncurrent liabilities and equity. (106)

Perpetual inventory: A record that shows additions and deductions for an item of inventory and hence the amount on hand at anytime. With a perpetual inventory, *cost of sales* is the total of deductions from inventory during the period. (76)

Physical inventory: The amount of inventory currently on hand, obtained by making a physical count. (78)

Plant assets: All tangible, noncurrent assets except land. (89) For acquisition of plant assets, see p. 90. For sale of plant assets, see p. 98.

Pledge: (1) In a nonprofit organization, a promise to make a contribution in the future. (2) In any organization, specified collateral provided as security for a loan.

Plow back: To retain assets generated by profitable operations for investment in an entity.

Pooling-of-interests method: A method of accounting for a business combination. The assets and equity of the combining firms are added together to form a new balance sheet. This method is used only when one firm acquires another firm by issuing common stock and when certain other conditions are met. Other business combinations are accounted for by the *purchase method*.

Posting: The process of transferring transactions from the *journal* to the *ledger*. (42)

Precollected revenue: *Advances from customers*.

Preferred stock: Stock, the owners of which have a preferential claim over common stockholders for dividends and for assets in the event of liquidation. (112)

Premium: The excess of the price received for a bond over its face value.

Prepaid expenses: The general name for intangible assets that will become expenses in future periods when the services they represent are used up. Example: prepaid insurance. (62)

Price-earnings ratio: The average market price of the stock divided by the earnings per share. (146)

Price-level-adjusted statements: Financial statements on which the amounts have been adjusted for changes in the value of the dollar from some specified base year. The amounts shown on such statements are said to be in dollars of constant purchasing power.

Primary financial statements: The income statement, balance sheet, cash flow statement, and (if needed) statement of changes in retained earnings. An entity's annual report consists of the primary financial statements plus notes and supplementary information.

Prime cost: The sum of direct materials cost and direct labor cost of a product.

Principal: (1) The amount of a loan that must be repaid. The total repayment consists of principal plus interest. (2) A person who employs an *agent*.

Prior period adjustment: An entry made directly to retained earnings to correct certain types of accounting errors made in prior periods. Such an entry is rare.

Process costing: A method of cost accounting that first collects costs by cost centers and then allocates the total costs of each center equally to each unit flowing through it during an accounting period. Contrast with *job-order costing*.

Product: Anything produced by an entity. Products may be either goods or services. (Some people use *product* to refer only to goods.)

Product cost: The direct materials, direct labor, and production overhead costs of a product. Contrast this with *period costs*. (84)

Production overhead cost: Product costs other than direct materials and direct labor. It includes, for example, supervision, building maintenance, and power. (84) See also *overhead rate*.

Profit: Another name for *income*.

Profit and loss statement: Another name for *income statement*.

Profit margin percentage: Net income expressed as a percentage of net sales. (143)

Profit-volume graph: A graph that shows the relationships among cost, volume, and profit, including the breakeven point.

Promissory note: A written acknowledgment of the amount that a borrower owes a creditor; a note receivable on the books of the lender and a note payable on the books of the borrower. (14)

Property, plant, and equipment: The term typically used on the balance sheet for tangible, long-lived assets. (90)

Proprietorship: An unincorporated business with a single owner. (22, 109)

Prorate: *Allocate*.

Prospectus: A document describing in great detail information about a proposed issue of securities and about the company that plans to issue the securities.

Provision for: A term used for an estimated liability or expense when the exact amount is not known. Example: provision for income taxes.

Purchase method: A method of accounting for a business combination. The acquiring firm adds the assets and liabilities of the acquired firm to its balance sheet. Assets are added at their fair value. If the purchase price exceeds the amount of acquired assets less liabilities, the excess is reported as *goodwill*. This method is used for all business combinations that do not qualify for the *pooling-of-interests method*.

Q

Qualified opinion: A form of an external auditor's opinion on financial statements that takes exception to one or more items reported thereon. Contrast this with *clean opinion*. (138)

Quick asset: Cash or a current asset that is readily convertible to cash; includes marketable securities and accounts receivable, but not inventory.

Quick ratio: Quick assets divided by current liabilities.

R

Ratio: The result of dividing one number by another.

Raw materials inventory: Goods on hand that will be used in producing a product.

Real account: An account for a balance sheet item; a *permanent account*; the opposite of a *nominal account*.

Real estate: Land, improvements to land, and natural resources on or in the land, but not structures.

Realization concept: Revenue is recognized when goods or services are delivered, in an amount that is reasonably certain to be realized. (50)

Receivable: An amount due from another entity. (14)

Receivables turnover: A ratio: total credit sales for the year divided by the amount of accounts receivable.

Recognition: The act of recording a revenue or expense item applicable to a given accounting period. Revenue recognition is governed by the *realization concept*. (51)

Red, in the: A colloquial term for operating at a loss.

Redemption: Paying the holder of a security earlier than the specified maturity date. If the price is higher than the price at maturity, there is a redemption premium.

Refunding a bond issue: Issuing new securities and using the proceeds to retire an existing bond issue.

Registered bond: A bond, the owner of which is recorded on the books of the issuing company. Payments are made to the registered owner. Contrast this with *bearer* bond.

Registration statement: A statement filed with the *Securities and Exchange Commission*, giving detailed information about the company.

Rental revenue: Revenue earned from permitting another party to use a building or other property. (53)

Repair cost: A cost incurred to restore a long-lived asset to good condition. Repair costs are not capitalized. Contrast this with *betterment*.

Report, Auditor's: *Opinion*.

Report package: Consists of a balance sheet for the beginning and end of the accounting period and an income statement for the accounting period. (70)

Research and development cost: Costs incurred in searching for new knowledge (research) or developing new or improved products or processes (development). Such costs are expensed as incurred.

Reserve: Formerly, used in the sense of "allowance," as an allowance for bad debts or *accumulated depreciation*; usage obsolete. Currently, used primarily as a segregated part of *retained earnings*, such as in reserve for contingencies.

Reserve recognition accounting: A method of accounting for discoveries of oil and gas resources. It capitalizes these resources at their realizable value; used only as supplementary information.

Residual claim: The claim of equity investors.

Residual value: The amount for which an entity expects to be able to sell a plant asset at the end of its service life. (92)

Retail method: A method of finding cost of sales when ending inventory at cost is not known. The amount is deduced by applying the normal markup percentage, adjusted for markdowns, to sales revenue.

Retained earnings: The increase in equity that has resulted from profitable operations; net income to date minus dividends to date. It is an equity item, not an asset. (18, 112)

Return on assets: A ratio: earnings before interest and taxes divided by net assets. Sometimes total assets is used rather than net assets. It may also be calculated on an aftertax basis and is equivalent to *return on permanent capital*.

Return on equity (ROE): A ratio: net income divided by the amount of shareholders' investment. (138)

Return on investment (ROI): A ratio that can mean either *return on owner's investment* or *return on permanent capital*. The meaning must be deduced from the context. (146)

Return on owner's investment: Another name for *return on equity*.

Return on permanent capital: A ratio: earnings before interest and taxes divided by total permanent capital (debt plus equity). It may also be calculated on an aftertax basis. (146)

Revenue: The increase in equity resulting from operations during a period of time, usually from the sale of goods or services. (30)

Royalty: A payment for the use of copyrighted or patented items; a payment for oil, gas, coal, or other natural resources. The amount is often calculated as a percentage of revenue or, in the case of natural resources, as a price per unit produced.

S

Salary: A form of compensation for personal services. Usually, salary refers to compensation of employees who are paid at a weekly or monthly rate, and *wages* to employees who are paid at an hourly or piece rate, but usage varies. (64)

Sale and leaseback: A transaction in which the owner of property sells it to another party and then leases it back from that party. Under some circumstances, this has income tax advantages.

Sales allowance: A reduction in the originally agreed-on price for goods or services, usually because the item is not fully satisfactory.

Sales discount: A reduction in the stated selling price, usually as a reward for prompt payment. Distinguish this from *trade discount*.

Sales income: Sometimes used to mean *sales revenue*. The term is misleading because income is the difference between sales revenue and expenses. (70)

Sales return: A reduction from sales revenue arising from goods returned by the buyer.

Sales revenue: Revenue from the delivery of goods or the performance of services. (70)

Salvage value: *Residual value.*

Scrap value: *Residual value.*

Securities and Exchange Commission (SEC): A federal agency that regulates security exchanges and requires information from companies whose securities are publicly traded. Although authorized to prescribe accounting standards, the SEC usually supports standards issued by the *FASB* and limits its own rules primarily to matters of disclosure.

Security: An instrument such as a stock or bond. Securities give the party that owns them valuable rights from the entity that issued them. (14)

Segment: A major component of an entity, usually a component that produces and sells a major product line. Publicly held entities are required to report revenues, operating expenses, and *identifiable assets* for each segment and also for each continent on which they operate.

Selling and administrative expenses: An overall category for all expenses other than those related to production.

Serial bond: A bond that matures on a specified date; part of a serial bond issue, with bonds maturing on a series of specified dates.

Service life: The period of time over which an asset is estimated to be of service to an entity. (91)

Service revenue: Revenue from the performance of services. (53)

Services: Intangible products. *Products* consist of tangible goods and intangible services.

Shareholder equity: The equity section of a corporation's balance sheet. (18, 109)

Shareholders: The equity investors in a corporation; also referred to as stockholders. (18, 109)

Shrinkage: The amount of goods that have been stolen or spoiled and hence are no longer in inventory. (78)

Simple interest: Interest calculated on the *principal* only. Contrast with *compound interest*.

Sinking fund: A fund established to provide money for the retirement of *bonds*.

Social Security taxes: Federal taxes on both employers and employees; used to provide retirement, health, and disability benefits to employees.

Sole proprietorship: *Proprietorship*.

Solvency: An entity's ability to meet its long-term obligations. Often measured by the *debt ratio*. (149)

Specific identification: Finding *cost of sales* by the cost of the specific item sold. (76)

Standard, financial accounting: A pronouncement of the Financial Accounting Standards Board. Entities are required to follow *FASB* standards in their general-purpose financial statements.

Standard cost: An estimate of what the cost of a product or process should be. Contrast with *actual cost*.

Stated capital: Amount of capital contributed by shareholders; *paid-in capital*.

Stated value: The amount at which *no-par-value stock* is reported on the balance sheet, as voted by the directors. (111)

Statement of cash flows: *Cash flow statement*.

Statement of financial position: Another name for a *balance sheet*.

Statement of Position (SOP): Guidance on an accounting issue published by the American Institute of Certified Public Accountants. An SOP does not have quite the authoritative force of an *FASB* standard, but entities are expected to be guided by it unless they have good reason to do otherwise.

Status report: A report of the state of assets and equity as of one moment in time; a balance sheet. (32)

Stock: See *capital stock, common stock, preferred stock*.

Stock appreciation rights: An incentive compensation plan in which the payment is related to the increase in the price of an entity's stock. These rights are similar to a stock option plan, but do not involve actual shares of stock.

Stock dividend: A dividend consisting of shares of stock in the corporation. (113)

Stock split: An exchange of the number of shares of stock outstanding for a substantially larger number. (113)

Stockholders: The owners of a corporation; also referred to as *shareholders*. (18, 109)

Straight-line depreciation: A depreciation method that charges off an equal fraction of the estimated *depreciable cost* of a plant asset over each year of its *service life*. (94)

Subchapter S Corporation: A corporation that has elected to be taxed as if it were a partnership. Also known as an S Corporation.

Subsidiary: A corporation that is controlled by another corporation (the *parent*). (117)

Successful-efforts accounting: Capitalization of drilling costs of only those wells that contain substantial amounts of oil or gas.

Sum-of-years'-digits depreciation: An accelerated depreciation method, no longer widely used.

T

T-account: The simplest format for an *account*. (35)

Take-or-pay contract: A contract in which the buyer agrees to pay a specified minimum amount whether or not goods were delivered or services provided during the period. Such a contract guarantees that the buyer will have rights to receive products (such as coal) if they are needed.

Tangible assets: Assets that can be touched; they have physical substance. Noncurrent tangible assets are often referred to as property, plant, and equipment. (15)

Tax depreciation: The depreciation method used in calculating taxable income. (99)

Taxable income: The amount of income subject to income tax, computed according to the rules of the IRS. For the difference between taxable income and accounting income, see p. 99. For taxable income with the LIFO method, see p. 81. For treatment of depreciation, see p. 99.

Temporary account: A revenue or expense account. A temporary account is closed at the end of each accounting period. (44) Contrast with *permanent account*.

10-K: The name of the report required annually by the SEC from all publicly traded companies. It is similar to a company's *annual report*, but contains more detailed information.

Time deposit: A savings account or similar account in a bank. A time deposit earns interest, but withdrawals may be subject to restrictions. Contrast with *demand deposit*.

Timing difference: A difference between net income as reported on the income statement and taxable income. It results from a transaction in the current period that is expected to have the opposite effect on income taxes in future periods. The difference between tax depreciation and accounting depreciation is the principal example.

Trade discount: A discount from a list price used to calculate the actual selling price. Sales revenue is reported at the ac-

tual price; the trade discount does not appear in the accounting records. Contrast with *sales discount*.

Trade-in: An asset that is given in part payment for another asset. Accounting treatment of a transaction involving a trade-in varies, depending on whether the new asset is similar or dissimilar to the asset traded in. See also *boot*.

Trademark: A word or symbol that distinctively identifies a product. It is an asset if purchased from another entity.

Transaction: An event that is recorded in the accounting records. (23)

Treasury stock: Previously issued stock that has been bought back by the corporation. (111)

Turnover: The number of times that inventory or accounts receivable are replaced during a year.

U

Uncollectible account: An account receivable that an entity believes will not be paid and therefore is *written off*. (54)

Unconsolidated subsidiary: An entity whose accounts are not included in a consolidated financial statement because the *parent* does not own more than 50% of its stock. (117)

Unearned revenue: *Advances from customers*.

Unexpired cost: The cost of assets on hand now that will be consumed in future accounting periods. (62)

Unissued capital stock: Stock that has been *authorized* but not yet *issued*.

Unrealized loss on marketable securities: An expense of the current period to the extent that the market value of a securities portfolio at the end of the period is less than its book value.

V

Value added: The cost of items, other than materials, that are used in the production process.

Variable cost: An element of cost that changes approximately in proportion to changes in volume. Contrast with *fixed cost.*

Variance: The difference between an *actual* amount and a *standard* or budgeted amount. Variances can be identified for revenues, expenses, and costs.

Vendor: A supplier from whom the entity acquires goods or services.

Vested benefit: An employee's benefit under a pension plan that does not depend on continued employment with the entity.

W

Wage: An amount earned for personal services rendered. This often refers to compensation of employees who are paid at an hourly or piece rate. See also *salary.*

Warrant: A certificate that entitles its owner to buy a specified number of shares of stock at a specified price.

Warranty: An implied or stated promise by the seller to repair or replace a defective product. Estimated future warranty pay-ments associated with products sold during the current period are an expense of the current period.

Wasting assets: Natural resources, such as coal, oil, and other minerals. The process of charging wasting assets to expense is called *depletion.* (101)

Withholding: An amount deducted by the employer from an employee's gross earnings and remitted to the IRS as advance payment on an employee's income tax. It also applies to amounts deducted from interest or dividend payments for a similar purpose.

Work in process inventory: The costs incurred to date on products for which production has begun but has not yet been completed. The product can be either goods or services.

Working capital: The difference between current assets and current liabilities. Sometimes it is used to refer to current assets, but this usage is confusing. (105, 125)

Write down: To reduce the cost of an item, especially inventory, to its market value. (83)

Write-off: To remove an asset from the accounts. For write-offs of accounts receivable, see p. 56.

Z

Zero-coupon bonds: A bond that does not pay interest. Investors pay less than the face amount for such a bond. Their return is the difference between the amount they pay and the principal, which is due at maturity. (108)